THE SORROWS OF FREDERICK

The Sorrows of Frederick

A PLAY BY

Romulus Linney

HARCOURT, BRACE & WORLD, INC.

NEW YORK

Copyright © 1966 by Romulus Linney

First edition

Library of Congress Catalog Card Number: 68-12581

Printed in the United States of America

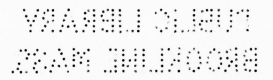

For Margaret Andrews Linney

for Mary Durant

and for all the actors who first played it

CONTENTS

CHARACTERS

FREDERICK II OF PRUSSIA, CALLED THE GREAT
The King / The Prince / The Boy

HIS FAMILY
Frederick William I, his father / Sophia Dorothea, his mother / Elizabeth Christine, his wife

HIS CABINET
The General / The Doctor / The Chancellor / The Bishop

HIS FRIENDS
A Lieutenant / M. G. Fredersdorf / Moreau de Maupertuis / Voltaire

HIS SUBJECTS
The Court-martialed Soldier / The Messenger / The Painter / The Historian / The Executioner / The Giant

Soldiers of the Prussian Army

PLACE
Prussia in the memory of Frederick the Great

TIME
1712 to 1786, his life span, during which many characters undergo various transformations in his consciousness

Overture

Empty stage, with a few low platforms. In the air, several screens tilted slightly down, and at center, one large screen. As the audience is being seated, portraits of Frederick the Great are projected, sometimes singly, sometimes simultaneously. One of his sonatas or concertos for flute is played while we see the portraits by Pesne, Chodowiecki, Menzel, and so on. As the figures of the King pass before us, we hear the voices of the actors of the evening.

Most history is a compilation of lies, mixed with a few truths.
—Frederick the Great, in his own *History of My Times*

Frederick II, called the Great, ruled Prussia for 46 years, from 1740 until 1786. He had been a sensitive youth but he made a strong king.

The last time I saw him, at a review, he came riding his big white horse, wearing a plain blue coat, quite threadbare, the front covered with Spanish snuff. His hat was very greasy, had lost one corner by a bullet, and had two holes in one side. Lurching forward in the saddle, he subjected his weary troops to a ferocious individual inspection.
—Latrobe, *Anecdotes of the Late King of Prussia*

A sad Creed, this of the King's; he had to do his duty without fee or reward. Yes, reader—and what is well worth your attention, you will have difficulty to find a King or a man who stood more faithfully to his duty. To poor Friedrich that was all the Law and all the Prophets.

—Carlyle, *Frederick the Great*

Nobody had the least suspicion that a tyrant of extraordinary military and political talents, of industry more extraordinary still, without fear, without faith, without mercy, had ascended the throne of Prussia. His selfish rapacity gave the signal to his neighbors. His example quieted their sense of shame. The whole world sprang to arms. On the head of Frederick is all the blood that was shed in a war that raged for many years.

—Macaulay, *Frederick the Great*

That the hero who unceasingly struggled through war, sacrificing the pleasures of life to maintain the honor of the kingdom, should still be held in high veneration of his subjects, is the best evidence of his greatness.

—Kugler, *Frederick the Great*

He possessed that ruthless, terrible Prussian directness. Frederick gave himself as he was and he saw things as they are.

—Treitsche, *History of Prussia*

Better be a eunuch in a Turkish harem than a Prussian subject.

—18th-century proverb

Frederick came to the throne when Prussia was an insignificant part of the Holy Roman Empire. He attacked Austria at once, and annexed the large province of Silesia. Acting as his own General, he fought many fierce battles in the several Wars of the Austrian Succession.

With the first dawn of morning, the two armies, in close contact, rushed furiously upon each other. There were seventy thousand on the one side and seventy-five thousand on the other. They faced each other in straight lines over a plain nearly ten miles in length. It is vain to give the reader an adequate idea of the terrible battle which ensued. With musketry, artillery, gleaming sabres and rushing horsemen, the infuriate hosts dashed each upon the other. At length, the Austrians, having lost nine thousand dead and wounded, seven thousand prisoners, sixteen thousand in all, retreated, bleeding and exhausted. Frederick remained the undisputed victor of the field. Five thousand of his brave soldiers lay dead or wounded upon the plain. Such was the battle of Hohenfriedberg, once of world-wide renown, now almost forgotten.

—Abbott, *History of Frederick the Great*

If you want an omelette, you must be prepared to break a few eggs.

—Frederick, table talk

The same discipline that allowed him to drench Europe in blood without one word of consent from a single subject also allowed him to improve a legal code, build schools, drain and ditch and hedge his countryside. How splendid a figure, had his cause been just.

—Lord Rosebery, *Frederick the Great*

Frederick the Great may visit us? Then at last I shall see a King.

—Madame de Pompadour

Madame de Pompadour? I never heard of her.

—Frederick

Frederick won his wars to keep Silesia. He found himself famous. He was a statesman, a general, a lawmaker, but also a philosopher, an historian, a fine flutist, a composer, and a poet. He built a beautiful retreat, named it Sans Souci, and held elegant dinner parties there, receiving many famous visitors.

I had been there only a short time when I saw him appear, followed by his reader and a pretty spaniel. As soon as he saw me, he came directly toward me. Lifting his hat and calling me by name in a thunderous tone, he asked me what I wanted, and demanded specific answers to questions about the army, navy, and treasury of Venice. After a broken conversation, during which he told me there was some truth in what I said, we arrived at a little garden gate. He stopped in front of me, and looked me over, up and down, from head to foot.

"Do you know that you are a good looking man?" he said.
    —Casanova

He rises at five in summer, six in winter. After a simple breakfast he plays the flute and thinks about philosophy and affairs of state. In the mornings he drills his troops. At noon, his meal is accompanied by conferences, and then matters of administration are very speedily accomplished. In the early evenings he will often attend or play in a concert with his musicians, scientists, poets and artists. At eight-thirty he has supper with his distinguished friends.
    —Thomas Campbell, *Frederick the Great*

Pee well and be cheerful; it's the best we can do on this earth. My hemorrhoids salute your gonorrhea.
    —Frederick to a friend

Do you know the story of the young man who, confessing his sins, his pleasures, his amorous intrigues to his father confessor, heard the latter exclaim at each item:

"What a dog of a life! Oh, what a dog of a life!"

"But Father," said the young man, "is it so great a crime to enjoy the pleasures of love, to seduce pretty girls, and to decorate the foreheads of those husbands unaware of the value of their wives? Must I, for joys so keen and of such short duration, suffer endless pain?"

"Oh, you wretch," said the Father Confessor, "it is not

your life I am talking about but my own! What a dog of a life!"

Mine, my dear sir, is just such a life.
—Frederick to his reader, Henri de Catt

Love is a little deity that spares no one. One way or another, he is sure of you.
—Frederick, table talk

His most famous visitor was Voltaire.

You are perhaps the greatest King who has ever lived.
—Voltaire

I was born too soon but I have no regrets, I have known Voltaire.
—Frederick

Voltaire, a great writer, is a man of the vilest and most contemptible character.
—Frederick

He always talks like a philosopher just before he acts like a king.
—Voltaire

If you do commit suicide, as you keep threatening, nobody, believe me, will call you a martyr. Is it worth pretending to be a philosopher, if you are unable to keep on living as a private man?
—Voltaire

He is a chaos of clear ideas.
—Frederick

This society reminds me of what the wolf said to the lamb: "You spoke ill of me last year. I must suck your blood."
—Voltaire

You make the mind laugh and the soul weep.
  —Frederick

M. Voltaire makes me understand perfectly all those things I do not wish to understand.
  —A lady of the French court

Should you look for the character of Voltaire among the journalists and illiterate writers of the age, you will there find him characterized as a monster, with a head turned to wisdom and a heart inclined to vice; the powers of his mind and the baseness of his principles forming a detestable contrast. But seek for his character among writers like himself, you will find him very differently described. You perceive him, in their accounts, possessed of good nature, humanity, greatness of soul, fortitude, and almost every virtue.
  —Goldsmith, *On the Death of Voltaire*

He prepared us for freedom.
  —The French people

Frederick was threatened by a coalition of Austria, Russia and France, who were determined to make him give up Silesia, and to destroy the new Prussia that was upsetting the balances of power. Frederick attacked first, and plunged Europe into the Seven Years' War.

Waves of blood are washing over the world, and the source of much of it is Frederick the Great. He came to the throne with a shrivelled heart and a sardonic scorn for all mankind: its morals, its conventions, its cant. There was little human left.
  —Lord Rosebery, Preface to de Catt's *Frederick the Great*

If there is anything to be gained by being honest, let us be honest; but if it is necessary to deceive, let us deceive.
  —Frederick

Impressions one receives in childhood cannot be erased from the soul.
—Frederick

He won, and again kept Silesia, but the price he paid was enormous, both in his own health and well-being, and in the lives and properties of his people. He worked hard to rebuild his nation.

You may serve him faithfully, always, but if you fail once, it is all for nothing. For the least thing, he will send you about your business after thirty years of service.
—Henri de Catt, *Memoirs of the King's Reader*

He interfered with everything. We can make shift to live under a debauchee or a tyrant, but to be ruled by a busybody is more than human nature can bear.
—Macaulay

Blessed are the absent, for they know not what is happening.
—Frederick

In his last years he held intensive Army maneuvers and continually inspected his kingdom. He withdrew from other people.

I am tired of ruling a nation of slaves.
—Frederick

Inarticulate notions, fancies, transient aspirations, he might have, in the background of his mind. One day, sitting for a while out of doors, gazing into the Sun, he was heard to murmur, "Perhaps I will be nearer thee soon"; and indeed, nobody knows who he meant or what his thoughts were in those final months. There is traceable only a complete superiority to Fear and Hope; in parts, too, are half-glimpses of

a great motionless interior lake of Sorrow, sadder than any
tears or complaining, which are altogether wanting to it.
—Carlyle, *Frederick the Great*

*His reputation through the years has been often disputed.
Some detest, but others admire.*

From *Ode to Death* by Frederick the Great

> See the world's victor mount his car;
> Blood marks his progress wide and far,
>   Sure he shall reign while ages fly,
> No: vanished like a morning cloud,
> The hero was but just allow'd
>   To fight, to conquer, and to die.
>
> And is it true, I ask with dread,
> That nations, heap'd on nations, bled
>   Beneath his chariot's fervid wheel?
> And now with trophies adorn the spot,
> Where his pale corpse was left to rot,
>   While hymns are sung and church bells peal?

Would I stand here, if you were still alive?
—Napoleon at the tomb of Frederick the Great

Prussia is a great Power, its position achieved by the tran-
scendent genius of Frederick the Great. Although he was not
untouched by personal ambition, his position in our past history must excite in every one of his successors the desire to
emulate him.
—Bismarck, *Reflections*

*Drum roll. The lights in the theater go out. On the cen-
ter screen we see photographs of Hindenburg and Hitler. It is March 21, 1933. They are bearing golden funeral wreaths for the coffins of Frederick the Great and
his father, Frederick William I. Drums. Newsreel pic-*

tures of this ceremony, which marked the founding of the Third Reich. We see Hitler standing inside the Garrison Church at Potsdam, reading his speech from a lectern to the seated Hindenburg, who is dressed in his Prussian uniform. Around them sit many figures in dazzling uniforms, others in brown shirts, wearing swastikas. Hitler wears a morning coat, looks stiff, awkward, and tentative. His voice is very quiet and reverent.

HITLER   In his name and in your honor, Herr General Field-marshal, we have come to this place sacred to the history of our nation. Here, today, we call into existence the Third Reich. For here, beneath our feet, lies the glorious tomb of Frederick the Great, and nowhere else may we better celebrate the grandeur of the past and the fresh strength of the present. May Providence grant to our generation that courage and endurance we all inherit, here at the shrine of our greatest King.

(The figures fade into darkness.)

Act 1
The Prince

(We hear a ghostly subject played on a harpsichord: the opening notes of Bach's "Musical Offering," a theme given him by Frederick.

At center, lights reveal an old man, asleep on a narrow iron cot. He is propped up in a sitting position. Suffering from dropsy, he wheezes, coughs, twists about on the brutal iron cot. His head is tied up grotesquely in a white handkerchief. Next to the cot, a small table and one chair, over which lies a faded, stained, blue Prussian uniform coat.

The spectral notes of the "Musical Offering" fade away. Silence. The old man writhes, twisting about in his sleep. He calls out for someone whose name we cannot hear. Still asleep, he suddenly sits upright, and holds out his arms with yearning. His eyes are closed.)

FREDERICK   No? No? Not at all? Oh . . . Well, there you are! I thought so. Come along, then. Come on. Come on.

(He smiles, embraces the air, and falls back on the cot, murmuring gently, clasping his phantom in his arms. A soldier comes to the bed, with a snare drum in his hands. He stands for a moment, looking at his watch. He puts it in his pocket, then beats the drum, in a savage tattoo. On the screen, a picture of a parade ground. Frederick the Great lurches up from his bed. He stands shivering as the apparition of his dream fades from his arms. The soldier steps back, and lowers the drum.)

SOLDIER   Five o'clock.

(Frederick nods. The soldier turns and receives from another soldier a plain copper basin and a towel, which he puts on the table, and then leaves. Frederick unties the handkerchief from his head, dabs his hands into the basin, flicks a few drops of water on his face. He coughs, spits, then suddenly stops and stands very still, cocking his head to one side, as if listening for something intently. We hear a very coarse voice.)

VOICE   The Prince will be up, dressed, and ready for the tasks before him within seven minutes from the instant he opens his eyes. He will consume his breakfast in three minutes. He will organize his person in four, and take up his duties in one. From bed to parade ground, not one second more than a quarter of an hour.

(From the first word of the voice, Frederick has moved through his morning toilet with rigid haste. The soldier has come in with a steel tray. Frederick sits on the edge of his cot, clutching a sheaf of papers. He reads, wolfs rolls and coffee from the tray, and has his boots put on, all at the same time.)

FREDERICK   Are they all here?

SOLDIER   Yes, your majesty.

FREDERICK   All right. The General and the Lieutenant.

(The soldier leaves. Frederick flops a short, dirty wig on his head, adjusts it carelessly. He is ready for his day, needing only to put on his uniform coat to be dressed, for he has slept in his trousers and underclothes. The uniform is old, and in one conspicuous place it is patched.

His boots are unpolished, the leather dry and mottled.
He is a strange figure: an old man, very frail and short,
bent, his teeth gone, his mouth twisted, his body caked
with dirt under the patched, faded, stained uniform. He
sits on the cot, lays his long sword in a glittering silver
scabbard across his knees, and looks over his papers
fiercely. The General and the Lieutenant enter. They are
dressed in dazzling Prussian uniforms, in bizarre con-
trast to Frederick. They stand in frozen attention be-
fore their King, who keeps on looking at his papers.)

FREDERICK   Well, gentlemen?

GENERAL   Sire, Baron Heinrich Nocklin-Grantz has the
honor to present his son, Lieutenant in your Majesty's
Death's Head Hussars. The Baron has asked me to
speak for his progress as an officer, in view of his proposed
marriage to the eldest daughter of the house of Larnbach.

FREDERICK   And do you, General?

GENERAL   I beg your pardon, Sire?

FREDERICK   Speak for him.

GENERAL   Your Majesty, while I firmly uphold the tradition of celibacy among the Death's Head Hussars, I also
present my unqualified approval of this young man's
performance of his duties.

FREDERICK   And what does that mean?

GENERAL   Why, that I heartily approve of his achievements
as an officer.

FREDERICK   Grantz isn't an old friend, General?

GENERAL   Yes, of course, Sire. A distinguished friend.

FREDERICK   So. Grantz-Larnbach. Fat dowry, adjoining estates. Perfection, except for the trifling obstacle of the Hussars. Well, how's the girl? Bearable, young man?

LIEUTENANT   Yes, your Majesty.

FREDERICK   Wonderful. Now what, General? A transfer from the Hussars?

GENERAL   I would heartily approve that, Sire.

FREDERICK   *(Sharply)*   Yes, but do you propose it?

GENERAL   *(Very uneasy)*   Your Majesty, if your Majesty declares himself in favor of this matter, then I hope it may be so; if not, why, then, your Majesty doubtless knows what he is about, in my opinion.

FREDERICK   *(Disgusted)*   Nice to know you finally have one. Gentlemen, we need brave officers, not fat estates.

(He takes a long look at the Lieutenant.)

Young man, allow me to instruct you, your nervous commanding officer, and your distinguished father: A Prussian Hussar does not seek his fortune through the vagina, but by the sword! Your request is denied, I bid you both good morning.

(They salute and leave. Frederick studies another paper. The soldier enters.)

FREDERICK   Send in the new doctor.

(The soldier leaves. Frederick takes a jeweled snuffbox from his pocket, jams snuff into his nose, sneezes vio-

lently, wipes his nose with his hand. We see why his coat is stained. The Doctor enters.)

FREDERICK   Well, sir, you come in a long and honorable tradition. One more doctor to try and keep this old man alive. Let me tell you that he suffers from dropsy, gout, and a moldering disposition. Campfires blaze all day in his chest, and last night he took three cups of blood from God knows how many hemorrhoids. What do you think?

DOCTOR   That I see before me a stouthearted old man whose spirit seems healthy. It often rules the body, Sire.

FREDERICK   A healthy spirit! You don't know what you are talking about. Here you are, come from medical college, with your pockets no doubt filled with intestines, scrotums, and lungs, to treat me. But what, really, do you know about suffering, Doctor? How many graves have you filled?

DOCTOR   *(Coolly)*   Not as many as your Majesty.

FREDERICK   Well, I see *you* have a healthy spirit, anyway. Decipher this riddle: What part of an old King would you bleed to save a new nation?

DOCTOR   The heart. But it is fatal.

FREDERICK   My dear Doctor, what a shame you didn't go into the Army. It would be a pleasure to have you about in the field. Now, can you keep me from constipating myself with eel pie, and eating too many spices, dangerous passions in the strict days of old age?

DOCTOR   No, your Majesty.

FREDERICK   Oh?

DOCTOR   I cannot overcome the nature of the King of Prussia. But when he collapses, I will get him on his feet again.

FREDERICK   Then you have your appointment. I promise to take your pills and sip all your brews. Good morning.

(The Doctor leaves. The soldier appears.)

FREDERICK   Chancellor.

(The soldier leaves. The Chancellor enters, fat and frightened.)

FREDERICK   Good morning. I have investigated your monthly depositions and I have approved three verdicts against five of your district administrations. You were all wrong about that tax proclamation at Magdeburg. Two of your acreage allotments are incorrect. You are wrong about the depth of the wine barrels in Küstrin, and about the new method of shearing sheep. Well?

CHANCELLOR   I cannot defend myself. I . . . I did the best I could.

FREDERICK   I know that. Please stop shaking. I'm not going to shoot you. The rest of your effort seems capable, only lacking in detail. I require full particulars, always! I have corrected part of your deposition. Here. Now, let me watch you study it.

(Frederick peers over the Chancellor's shoulder as he studies the paper.)

VOICE OF A BOY   But my father is the King. His figures always tally. He is the King.

VOICE OF A MAN   Prince, he knows his kingdom. Wine to the last flagon, sheep's wool to the hair, bookkeeping to the last decimal. How much spent for ink in the inkpot of a city clerk. How often to reshingle a roof. How many strokes of a hammer to drive one nail.

VOICE OF A BOY   His addition is always slightly unreadable. I refuse to salute his impossible industry. But he is my father, and I love him.

FREDERICK   Do you see? Here. And here.

CHANCELLOR   Yes, yes, your Majesty. That is the way it should be done.

FREDERICK   Then do it that way. Good morning.

(The Chancellor leaves. The soldier appears.)

FREDERICK   The Bishop.

(The soldier leaves. The Bishop appears, white-haired, kindly, and firm.)

FREDERICK   *(With great charm)*   I am delighted to see you, my dear friend. My apologies for this miserable hour, but I have to fight today, and we must chat a bit first. You are looking extremely well.

BISHOP   I am very happy to see your Majesty.

FREDERICK   Good. Well, the Holy Ghost and I have agreed that the prelate Fuhlweisse will be coadjutor of Breslau. We have mutually decided that you and all your brothers in Christ who oppose him will be looked upon as offering blasphemous resistance to the Holy Ghost.

BISHOP   This great understanding between your Majesty
and the Holy Ghost is something new. I did not know
you were even acquainted with him. Fuhlweisse is not
acceptable.

FREDERICK   Oh, I think God made donkeys, Doric columns,
and Kings, to bear the burdens of this earth, while stating
plainly that the kingdom of Christians is not of this
world. Now why can't holy men leave it like that and
stop trying to change it all about? You have always been
more sensible than your scheming brothers in Christ.
Help me keep them from complicating the machinery of
the State. Relent, relent.

(Pause. No response)

You know, I envy you the heavenly Jerusalem you win
for yourself. I will doubtless not qualify. My nature
has become sour here in the backwaters of age and re-
sponsibility. I would surely make an impossible angel.

(Pause. No response)

On the other hand, I insist about Fuhlweisse, and I do
not shake with fear at holy displeasure, as my father
did.

BISHOP   Oh, your Majesty, you are a thousand times greater
than your father, God rest him. But Fuhlweisse is not
acceptable.

FREDERICK   You are about to cause yourself a great deal
of trouble. I promise that Fuhlweisse will have nothing
to say about the Church. He will only deal with civil
authorities. If he gets out of hand, martyr him.

BISHOP   He is not acceptable.

FREDERICK   Then I will martyr you. Reread your sacred history. It is not difficult. I can have your ring tomorrow

and give it to my dogs to sharpen their teeth on. Come now, in the name of a reasonable God, I support the Church like a timid monk, you let me have Fuhlweisse where I want him.

BISHOP   Do you really believe I serve the Church of Martin Luther with scorn, that I don't know your tolerance is nothing but contempt? Or that I am so large a fool that I will stand here bantering with a determined King? I put my trust in God. Fuhlweisse is not acceptable. Martyr us both, if you can.

FREDERICK   I shall do my best. If you insist upon hanging from a cross, I will nail you up there. Good morning.

(The Bishop turns to leave.)

FREDERICK   Well, wait a minute!

BISHOP   Yes?

FREDERICK   We are both very old. We should manage these things better, really. Everyone knows that at the eleventh hour I will crack my whip and you will jump. Can't we at least drop the pretense that we have any *faith* to fight about?

BISHOP   It is not a pretense, Sire.

FREDERICK   Can't do it, can you? Poor man, you just can't do it. Will you then still maintain with me that the soul and the body are two separate commodities? Come, now. Do you insist on preserving that decayed belief?

BISHOP   I do.

FREDERICK   How?

BISHOP   By memory. Does not the King remember the faith of the Prince?

FREDERICK   No.

BISHOP   I beg you to try.

FREDERICK   Absurd. You would define religious faith as something remembered? Something recalled from youth, like a boy's vision of love?

BISHOP   Exactly. It has to be, at our age.

(He leaves. Frederick stares after him. We hear the voice of a young boy.)

VOICE   When my dear Papa must die, will he live in heaven? And when I must die, will I live there with him, on and on forever, after our bodies perish?

FREDERICK   *(Aloud)*   Ridiculous! Thank God.

(The soldier appears.)

FREDERICK   Court-martial. The accused and the General.

(The soldier leaves. Frederick studies his papers. The General and a private soldier enter. The private soldier is very short, a stocky peasant standing barely five feet tall. He is very slow-witted, but he holds himself straight, ready to accept his fate.)

FREDERICK   I am interested in this man, General. Please bear with me. Name?

PRIVATE SOLDIER   Johan Fredersdorf, your great eternal Majesty.

FREDERICK   Majesty is enough, never mind the stuffing. Are you from Silesia?

PRIVATE SOLDIER   No, your Majesty.

FREDERICK   Then you are no relation to an old man named Michael Gabriel Fredersdorf?

PRIVATE SOLDIER   No, your Majesty.

FREDERICK   I am sorry to hear it. He looked just like you. Same size, everything. He was a great friend, when I was young and needed one. Dead now. Fredersdorf, poor old thing. My God, how I miss him.

(Frederick begins to weep openly. The General stares at him.)

FREDERICK   *(Crying)*   How good he was! What a fine man he was! Don't distress yourself, General. I weep but I win! Oh, but really, really, you both should have known him. Fredersdorf, oh, Fredersdorf!

PRIVATE SOLDIER   Yes, your Majesty?

(Frederick stares at him, laughs violently, wipes his eyes.)

FREDERICK   Oh, not you, for God's sake! Well, well, court-martial. Something we can't cry away or laugh away. Is it, gentlemen?

PRIVATE SOLDIER   No, your Majesty.

GENERAL   No, your Majesty.

FREDERICK   I'm glad we all agree. You were the President of the Court, General. Correct?

GENERAL   It is, Sire.

FREDERICK   And you approve this verdict?

GENERAL   Without hesitation.

FREDERICK   I see. Well, soldier, you have been sentenced to death by hanging for having sexual relations with your horse.

(Pause)

Did you have sexual relations with your horse?

PRIVATE SOLDIER   Yes, your Majesty.

FREDERICK   A mare, I hope?

PRIVATE SOLDIER   Yes, your Majesty.

FREDERICK   Still, it's shocking.

(He peers at the soldier, noticing with fascination how very short the man is.)

Tell me, what did you stand on?

PRIVATE SOLDIER   A bucket, your eternal Majesty. It fell over.

FREDERICK   *(Chuckling)*   The bucket or the horse?

PRIVATE SOLDIER   The bucket.

FREDERICK   Harrowing. Nevertheless, you have been condemned to death because of it. Do you know any reason why I should change that?

(The private soldier stares stupidly at the King. He sinks to his knees as Frederick writes something on the court-

martial papers, hands them to the General, and then stands looking down at the soldier. After a moment, Frederick reaches down and cuffs him on the ear.)

FREDERICK   Verdict.

GENERAL   *(Reads)*   Pardoned. Transferred to the infantry.

(The soldier scrambles back to his feet, saluting awkwardly.)

PRIVATE SOLDIER   Thank you, thank you, your great eternal Majesty!

(Frederick nods, and the private soldier runs out. Frederick gazes quietly after him.)

FREDERICK   I am only sorry you must lose your horse.

(He wheels about, sharply.)

All right, General, I can guess your thoughts. What would have happened had his name been Schmidt?

GENERAL   He'd have been shot.

FREDERICK   I'm glad you have a logical mind. Now be so good as to relax a moment. Please sit on my cot. Thank you. Please don't sulk. Thank you.

(Frederick studies the General, who sits stiffly, outraged at such treatment.)

This is your first field command with me. We all know your reputation from Spain and France. You are a famous warrior. No man alive honors that condition more than I do, for I am one myself. But let us remember what we owe to our own blunders as we achieve all our glory, and keep careful track of small affairs, for they are very instructive. Agreed?

GENERAL   Yes, your Majesty.

FREDERICK   Bravo. Well, you were all fudge and pasty pudding about that marriage. You weren't sure what I would think about it. You fretted about me. A mistake. You made a decision and you accept the consequences, General; I will do the maneuvering. That's how *that* works. Yet you decide the dreadful fate of a blockheaded soldier with his brains in his britches, condemn him to death without hesitation. You were vague when you should have been decisive and decisive when you should have been vague. I hope you don't fight the way you think. Now, then. Will we win today?

GENERAL   Your Majesty, I am not a parrot. I will fight for you today until I conquer or fall. Victory is likely, that is all I have to say.

FREDERICK   Better. I have a slight glimpse of backbone. Well, you are wrong, of course, but for the right reason. We will win. Well, let's see. Anything you would like to know before we review the Army?

GENERAL   As a matter of fact there is. Where, your Majesty, are we going to meet the enemy?

FREDERICK   Can you keep a secret?

GENERAL   Of course.

FREDERICK   So can I.

   (He laughs.)

   Agreed?

(The General rises, very much insulted.)

GENERAL   As your Majesty desires.

FREDERICK   Man, you are stiff as a poker. We aren't getting
along too well, you and I. You're not very good at small
talk, General.

GENERAL   Perhaps that is because there is an army arrayed
outside, waiting for me to lead it into battle.

FREDERICK   Possibly. But that army out there is the Army
of Prussia, and it is waiting for me, not for you. My father created it, I perfected it. Now, I know you are going
to earn your enormous salary, but please realize the limits
of your commission. They'll wait, don't you think?

GENERAL   Certainly, Sire.

FREDERICK   Yes. Now, as long as we are being so intimate,
have I ever shown you this?

(He takes a gilded snuffbox from his coat.)

GENERAL   Exquisite. A beautiful thing.

FREDERICK   Notice the little specks of black ivory, and the
tiny jeweled hinges. This is the way it opens. Snuff?

GENERAL   Thank you, no.

FREDERICK   Do you know what it is?

GENERAL   I have heard it is opium.

FREDERICK   Just enough to kill me. An oral of gold and
eighteen little pills, and they ease my wretched mind so

much, so much. But some less lethal snuff, surely we need it. Here!

(He takes out another snuffbox. They pinch, salute each other, put it in their nostrils and sneeze, the General with careful delicacy, Frederick with appalling sloppiness.)

GENERAL   Ah. Good. Very good.

FREDERICK   My father tried to hang me once, when I was a child. He did it behind a large velvet curtain, with a sash. My mother cut me down. When I take snuff, and sneeze, the relief is like that. Like being unhung, if you follow me.

GENERAL   Indeed, yes.

FREDERICK   Indeed, no, General. What do you know about it? You were not the bullied child set out on a parade ground at the age of three!

(He holds up the opium snuffbox and then the other one.)

One to ease my body, and another to ease my mind. If there is no heaven, at least here is final peace and permanence. How I long for that.

(He strikes a pose and declaims.)

Oh Germans! Your intestinal wars and your broils,
The frenzies of your wraths clutch you in their toils!

(He looks at the amazed General and laughs.)

Well, not so good as Voltaire, no, but then Voltaire never composed verses on the morning of a fight, did he? Poetry, General, and a pillbox of deadly opium. That's the way I lull the poor child within me, keep him from crying, and send him to war and sleep.

(Suddenly, explosively)

Children should not be punished, General! Remember that! They will learn consequence without punishment! They will! Do you believe that?

GENERAL   Certainly, Sire.

FREDERICK   Do you beat your children?

GENERAL   I have none.

FREDERICK   Oh. Well, God knows that's not the answer. All right, then.

(He buckles on his sword and takes up his large hat.)

Have they learned to play my march yet?

GENERAL   Yes, your Majesty.

FREDERICK   How do you like it?

GENERAL   It is absolute perfection, Sire.

FREDERICK   All right, all right.

(The General salutes and leaves. Frederick stands thinking. He is seventy-three years old: bent, crabbed, impossible, with a lined and sallow face, a cruel mouth, and sulphurous eyes.)

FREDERICK   Let me see. Now let me see.

The ox must plow the furrow,
The nightingale sing afar,
The dolphin swim, O innocence,
And I—I must make war!

(Frederick's Hohenfriedburg "Victory March" is heard, played by a strident military band.)

Not bad. On the morning of a fight, that's not so bad.

(He listens to the music, smiles slightly, and steps off the platform, which moves offstage. He stands waiting, facing upstage. On the screen, in quick succession, a series of military etchings, ending with one of a regiment in review formation, which holds. Frederick waits. Onto the stage, slowly, moving to a point just under the screen, comes a large, grotesque framework of boards: split, splintered, held up by braces and props, but unmistakably the shape of a great horse. A military saddle sits on its back, with shining stirrups, and long reins reach from the distorted wooden head to the saddle. It is as if a gigantic hobbyhorse has somehow grown into a terrible old age. The horse is mounted on a rolling platform, and as it reaches the center, the General moves to one side, stands at attention, while a hussar with a battle flag stands at the other. With a lurch, walking with thumping, iron-heeled steps, Frederick stomps to his immense horse, and with awkward but stern tenacity, swings up into the saddle, and gathers in the reins. On the screen, the faces of soldiers at attention)

FREDERICK   Soldiers! I speak to you today as I have many times before. We are going to fight today, as we have many times before. We are going to fight Austrians, as we have many times before. We have a clear day. So we will soon see the bright sunlight shining on retreating Austrian rumps, as we have many times before. You stand now where your fathers stood, and your grandfathers, once more to follow your queer and upstart old King into battle. Let me tell you something about the commanding General of the Army we are going to demolish. He is a clotheshorse. His wardrobe fills four rooms. He owns, believe me, one thousand five hundred wigs. He would be the absolute delight of all the empresses and royal courtesans who surrounded us years ago, when we were nothing, and so haughtily demanded our obedience. They are no longer with us, poor ladies, but if they were, they would certainly count on this gentleman to deliver us up to them, hacked apart, with his perfumed hands. Look at our enemies with me! The world sees glitter and power. What do I see? Yesterday, a closetful of whores; today, a prancing clotheshorse! One thousand five hundred wigs, but no head! Well, soldiers, are we women in Prussia? Or are we tiny tots, with curling hair and pink toes? Are we the wood from which frightened children, bashful boys, and milksop husbands are carved? Are you the sons of your fathers? Soldiers?

(A great roar of soldiers. Frederick holds up his sword, stands in his stirrups.)

Now let me see bright sunlight on Austrian rumps! Show me bayonets! Into their lungs! Up their noses! Give me their ribs and their bellies and the shreds of their fat Austrian assholes! Follow your King and save your nation! Which one of you would live forever?

(Cannonade. A roar of soldiers. The crashing chords of the "Victory March." On the screen, soldiers marching.
   Quickly, out of breath, moving across the forestage, come two dust-stained soldiers, one of them the messenger. They move directly toward Frederick, paying no attention to anyone. They salute the King, and the messenger holds up a pouch. Frederick glares at him, reaches down and takes the pouch, opens it, takes out a letter, tosses the pouch to the soldier, who catches it and kneels. Frederick tears open the letter and reads it, quickly. Suddenly, his warlike fury vanishes. He slumps down in the saddle, crushing the letter to his chest. The roar of the soldiers, the cannonades, the "Victory March," all reach a chaotic

climax. Frederick holds one thin arm up into the air. Everything stops. The screen goes blank. The music is cut short.)

FREDERICK   *(Very quietly)*   Tell them I will be there to-morrow night. Have everything prepared. Don't stop to breathe. I'll be right behind you. Fly.

(The soldiers salute, and go off, quickly.)

FREDERICK   General. Call them back.

GENERAL   What?

FREDERICK   Call back the Army. Make camp and fortify it. We will not attack today.

GENERAL   That's impossible! Your Majesty, the enemy is in sight! We have no choice! We must attack! Now!

(Frederick begins to weep. High on his wooden horse, he slumps and sobs. The General watches him for a moment with revulsion.)

GENERAL   I must inform your Majesty that if we do not attack now as planned, I must resign my commission. I have never in all my career deserted a battlefield!

FREDERICK   *(Crying)*   I won't lose your battle, General.

GENERAL   *(Disgusted)*   Well, win it then.

(He turns on his heel and walks away. Frederick looks down at him with quick rage.)

FREDERICK   Come back here, you stupid pig.

(Amazed, the General turns and simply stares at him. Frederick crawls down from the saddle.)

FREDERICK   Forgive me, forgive me. You see me like a dog, biting into a stone. My whole life, General, is a battlefield, and I have just received a wound. I forget how to treat my officers, who are loyal and brave, as you are. Accept my apologies and bear with me.

GENERAL   Then what shall we do, Sire?

FREDERICK   Encamp the Army. Boldly. Parade a battalion about. Make odd movements and stage unreasonable arrivals. The Austrians will spend a week wondering what we are up to. They won't attack. I know them. Listen, General. How many times this same thing has happened to me! Forward march! The band plays, the battle flags are lifted, guns spit fire and iron, the soldiers roar and scream, we charge into smoke and flame, and, covered with blood, we are dying, all is lost, and then, victory! We win! Allelujah, General! *Te Deum!* And disaster strikes me! Always, always. It's my curse. My sister, my darling sister, my brother, my mother, my dear teacher Duhan, Fredersdorf, Voltaire, all died as I marched about victorious, and the news always came to me at moments of triumph! What a dog of a life! My casualties are those I love the most! My victories destroyed, my achievements mocked. I thought it was over, finished. There was no one left for me to mourn, but there is, there is!! It has come upon me again. Oh, God!

GENERAL   Your Majesty, what has happened? Who has been lost?

FREDERICK   *(Holding up his snuffbox of opium)*   No one that you would know. We try to save them by saying everything is eternal, but it is all finished at death. I am an old man, sick at heart. God knows I have the right to be. Stop fretting, General, about your military reputation. I will come back soon enough and polish it for you.

GENERAL You are leaving?

FREDERICK Do you mind?

GENERAL Your Majesty.

(Words pour out of Frederick, in a torrent, as his thoughts leap from one thing to another.)

FREDERICK Encamp the Army. I leave it in your hands, God help me. Be good enough to have it here when I return. Fire one shot without me and I will hang you up by your hair! Oh, I don't mean to insult you, sir. Forgive me. It's difficult for you to understand an old wretch like me. Generals are very brave, but so limited. Oh, where is Fredersdorf? And Voltaire, that monkey! They would know what is killing me!

GENERAL I am not insulted. I think I would rather lose this battle than see you so distressed. But who, your Majesty, is dead? Who?

FREDERICK Ah, this damned letter! Why did I live to receive it? Three horses, three, shot from under me. My snuffbox once stopped a piece of shell an inch away from my heart. A hundred powder burns, a thousand whines past my ear. Why not just one little lead bullet, here, into the brain of the King? Ludicrous! Ridiculous! No, General, I am not a madman. I have great claims to that, but, damnation, I'm sane enough.

(He puts away the snuffbox, takes deep breaths, stands as straight as he can.)

All right, encamp the Army. I will leave, for home, now. I will return in two days, at most. Everyone will think it is strategy of the most sublime brilliance. The truth, General? Well, an old man is going to his home to attend a funeral. And going right now. On horseback, send the carriage after me. Oh, the devil! The devil!

GENERAL   What can I say to you, Sire? Your loss must be terrible, to cause you such anguish.

FREDERICK   You think so? And you wonder what it is? Well, General, I leave the field for the most preposterous reason in the world, a broken heart. What do you think of that? Laughable. For this! This!

(He holds up the letter in a dramatic pose.)

For this I desert the field! Oh, my father. How flabbergasted you would be, faced with the soldier your son became, finally. Little fop, mincing about on his toes. With his warm gloves, his silks, and his concerts on the flute. Who all the same outfought Austria, Russia, and France, while you never left the parade ground! But today, you would vomit. After all my glory, today I run away. And the only wound I display is absurd at my age, a cracked heart. How that would revolt you! Rage and kick your heels if you must. Scream at the angels and stamp your feet, it doesn't matter. I will leave the field!

(He goes to the great horse, hooks one foot into the shining stirrup.)

Oh grief, mount behind me as always, and gallop home with me.

(He swings up into the saddle.)

What infernal company!

(Blackout. Drums, sharply, at the rhythm of a canter. The stage is cleared, leaving Frederick alone, mounted on

his wooden horse. On the screen above him, dimly, a large moving shadow of an old man on a horse, riding furiously, movements heavily exaggerated, a savage caricature of age and desperation, the old man's bony shoulders heaving, his thin arms spiderlike, his scrawny neck bobbing with the forward lunge of the horse, as though riding down into hell. A small spotlight slowly illuminates Frederick's face, where he sits on his horse beneath the screen, going home. Above him, the shadow, galloping, then the drumbeats fade away, and then the shadow. Light comes up on the forestage, where we see a small blue snare drum, with a red ribbon tied to it. A handsome little boy, six years old, walks to the drum. He is dressed in a miniature Prussian uniform. He sits down by the drum, plays with it. On his horse, looming above the child, Frederick watches him. The boy begins to beat the drum, playfully and aimlessly at first, then finding a rhythm, the cantering rhythm of the shadow. He taps it out, and the shadow of the horse and the old man riding appears again. We hear the coarse voice of Frederick William.)

FREDERICK WILLIAM   The Prince of Prussia shall be raised to manhood with the utmost care.

(He belches.)

His little pink fists, when they can grasp and hold, will handle drums and small weapons. Those dainty legs will be wrapped round with good strong leather boots. That pouting face will be exposed to wind and snow, and the harsh adversities that forge a man's aspect.

(He belches.)

(The little boy taps the drum, but slower, and the shadow fades. As Frederick William continues, from the darkness appear the General, the Lieutenant, the Chan-

cellor, the Doctor, the Bishop, the private soldier, and the giant, a man seven feet tall, in uniform, carrying a rifle. They take up positions in an ominous circle around the boy.)

FREDERICK WILLIAM A squeaking voice will learn to thunder the commands of the battlefield. Blank little eyes will see into the joints and bulwarks of the state. That unclear little blot of a mind will learn the dutiful worship of Almighty God, and the severe obligations of those who must rule a kingdom.

(The boy stops tapping. He looks up and sees the figures surrounding him. The screen goes blank. On his horse, a small spotlight on his face, Frederick smiles grimly.)

GENERAL I will supervise all your training.

BISHOP I will instruct your soul, and teach you how to save it.

LIEUTENANT I will teach you to stand up straight, and to ride a horse at full gallop.

DOCTOR I will prescribe your diet, and read you classical history.

CHANCELLOR I will teach you arithmetic and the art of practical affairs.

GIANT I will drill you, and drill you, and drill you.

PRIVATE SOLDIER I will polish your little boots, and take you out to play in the afternoons.

(The boy looks at them, frightened.)

BOY   Papa? Papa?

*(On the screen appears the face of Frederick William,
his own self-portrait, painted while he was sick in bed.
By his own vision, he is a tormented man, with a pinched
yet gross face, and suffering eyes.)*

VOICE OF FREDERICK WILLIAM   Welcome, son. Welcome, Prince,
to the duties of life.

*(All the figures bow, and retire. Into the light sweeps
a colorfully dressed, beefy woman, his mother, the Queen,
Sophia Dorothea. She is very nervous, and continually
looks about as if constantly afraid of being overheard.
The portrait of Frederick William remains above them
all.)*

QUEEN   Fritz, Fritz, let me see you! Yes, very nice. A nice
man is going to paint a pretty picture of you and your
sister, so don't get wrinkled. When he's finished, we'll
send the pretty picture off to your uncle who is King
of England. My family there loves you, Fritz; they do.
They will see how charming you and your sister are.
Won't that be nice? Then they will want you both.

*(She smiles, almost laughing. The boy runs into her
arms. She embraces him fondly, but continues to speak
as if they were both conspirators.)*

Be good now, darling, do what everyone tells you. Later
on, you see, you and your sister will marry into my family in England. We will have a wonderful time together.
You will be the king here, you see, your sister queen
there. We will all be so happy, and I won't have to live
here with your father. That's the way it will be, darling.
So nice, you'll see. But hush, not a word now. We will
have to wait a little while. Not long, just a little while,
not long.

(She has moved away from him, hand on her mouth, into the darkness, whispering nervously.)

Hush, hush. Not a word. Hush.

(As she disappears, the picture of Frederick William fades. The boy looks about in fright and bewilderment. He is now all alone on a darkened stage, except for Frederick, the embodiment of his age and fate, who looks down at him from the wooden horse. Their eyes meet. The boy shivers, and rubs his arms.)

FREDERICK   Cold. I remember. There is a very pretty red ribbon on your drum, child. Play with that, as long as you can.

(The boy goes to the drum, looks at the ribbon a moment, then is overcome with dejection. He twists the ribbon about, and begins to cry.)

FREDERICK   *(Fiercely)*   Don't cry! Fredersdorf! Fredersdorf!!

(The private soldier, now Michael Gabriel Fredersdorf, enters quickly, goes to the boy, gets down on his knees with him.)

FREDERSDORF   Now now now now now now now. Boo hoo, boo hoo. What on earth's the matter? Tell me.

(The boy shakes his head.)

FREDERSDORF   Well, you can't just keep on crying forever, you know. If you do that, why, don't you know what will happen? Huh?

(The boy sniffs, shakes his head again.)

FREDERSDORF   All those tears will make a great big river, and it will be so big it will wash us all away, every soul. Then what will we do? Listen, I can't even swim. Can you? So what do we do now? What can we do with this great big river? Huh?

BOY   *(Interested now)*   Fish in it.

FREDERSDORF   *(Laughing)*   Well, that's right. That's true. So you can.

(On the wooden horse above them, Frederick's harsh, aged face has softened, and he looks down upon them with a soft and delicate smile.)

FREDERSDORF   Will you let me come with you? Can I fish in it, too?

BOY   *(Shaking his head gravely)*   No.

FREDERSDORF   I see. Well, what will you catch?

BOY   A whale.

FREDERSDORF   Oh, ho! A whale! All right, but once you catch yourself a whale, what will you do with it?

BOY   Keep it.

FREDERSDORF   Where?

BOY   In my room. In a tub.

FREDERSDORF   All right. What is it going to eat? What will you feed it?

BOY   Mushrooms.

FREDERSDORF   Very good. One by one, or a basketful at
once?

BOY   One by one.

FREDERSDORF   But a whale eats a lot of mushrooms. What
will we do? Wait! I just remembered. I know a place
where lots and lots of mushrooms grow. Enough to fill
up any decent whale, no matter how hungry he gets.
Shall we go there together, and pick mushrooms for your
fine whale?

(Delighted, the boy claps his hands.)

BOY   Yes! Yes! Right now!

FREDERSDORF   All right, away we go. But first you have to
have a decoration, so that everybody will know you are
King of the Mushrooms and can pick as many as you
like for all your whales. Here.

*(He takes the red ribbon and a silver ornament from the
side of the drum, makes a medal and ribbon out of them,
then decorates the boy gracefully.)*

There now!

*(They salute each other in fun, and start to go. But in
the darkness, the circle of the cabinet members has formed
again, and they move out and intercept them. They dis-
miss Fredersdorf with contempt. He bows and leaves,
and the boy looks after him with sorrow. The General
picks up the drum and taps it with his fingers.)*

GENERAL   Compose yourself, Prince!

*(The boy removes the ribbon, and gives it to the Gen-
eral. He squares his tiny shoulders and stands at attention.)*

LIEUTENANT   I have a fine pony for you to ride. He goes like the wind.

BISHOP   The holy Church has many enemies. It must always be on guard.

CHANCELLOR   Figures must march like soldiers. There is never an excuse for error.

DOCTOR   The government of ancient Persia is a fascinating place to begin our study.

GIANT   Attention! Forward, march!

(The General taps the drum, and the boy marches off with his captors. The drumbeat is taken up, and the shadow of the horse and rider appears again on the screen. On his horse, Frederick travels.

The Queen dashes onto the stage, regal in spite of her bulk. She carries a tiny fan, ludicrous in her large fist. Right behind her, choking on his anger, comes Frederick William.)

QUEEN   I thank God I have nothing to reproach myself with, unless it is loving you too much!

FREDERICK WILLIAM   Intrigues, treacheries, you are no better at it than I am. We are not diplomats, never will be. Don't play at it. I'm blunt and honest and I tell you nothing will happen in England. No marriages. Nothing nothing nothing. Never!

QUEEN   As you wish. We will all be pleased to remain here, to listen while you scream at your soldiers, and beat your children.

FREDERICK WILLIAM   Madam, you speak to the King of your nation. Be careful! I only warn you, be careful!

(On his horse, Frederick watches with shivering dis-
taste.)

QUEEN   What more do you want today?

FREDERICK WILLIAM   My son. My boy. The Prince! The little
monkey you have turned into a simpering fop. Where did
you get that miserable tutor to teach him Latin? That
man's lucky he's still alive!

QUEEN   You dismissed him?

FREDERICK WILLIAM   Yes, the bastard. Latin is a waste of
time. I won't have him corrupted by it.

QUEEN   How dare you? He was a distinguished and honorable man, who loved our son.

FREDERICK WILLIAM   *(Roaring)*   I dare because I am the
King. That man is a pedantic scribbler, and pedantic
scribblers shit ink!

QUEEN   Beast. Beast.

FREDERICK WILLIAM   And you're a deceitful bitch. Tell that
monkey there will be no concert tonight on that disgraceful flute. He comes to me tonight.

QUEEN   Vile, vile, vile.

FREDERICK WILLIAM   I know my duty to my son. By God,
you'll both of you find out what that is! You will! You
will!

(In fury, he aims a blow of his fist at the Queen, but
misses her, and stalks off.
She recoils, curses under her breath, stamps her foot

*in outraged frustration. She paces for a minute, stops,
thinks, mutters, then sees the man on the horse, who has
raised his sword above the scene he has witnessed.)*

QUEEN   Oh!

(Slowly, Frederick lowers his sword.)

FREDERICK   Forgive me. I did not mean to frighten you.

QUEEN   Do you belong here?

FREDERICK   Oh, yes. I belong here.

QUEEN   Well, you did frighten me. But you are obviously a
man of stature. You have the eye of a gentleman, sir.

FREDERICK   Thank you.

QUEEN   Do you have children?

FREDERICK   No.

QUEEN   Then you are spared a great deal of trouble. Are
you married?

FREDERICK   Yes. I do not often visit my wife.

QUEEN   You are spared even more. My husband would
envy you.

FREDERICK   That is an envy difficult for me to imagine.

(The Queen puts her hand to her eyes, and sways.)

FREDERICK   Do you feel all right?

QUEEN   No. Oh, that man! Beast! I loathe and despise him! Every ounce of his flesh, every hair on his body!

FREDERICK   Yes, of course. It explains your fourteen pregnancies nicely.

QUEEN   What? I have only been pregnant six times. You may be a gentleman, sir, but your comments are very wild and fanciful.

FREDERICK   Six, I beg your pardon. But time stretches ahead, and, as you say, it is dull in this brutal land.

QUEEN   Tonight my boy must go and sit with him. He must drink and smoke and keep those disgusting brutes company while they howl. He will be treated, oh, who knows how badly. He will despise us all, in time.

FREDERICK   You don't know that. Perhaps it will be less dramatic. He may simply be forced to do his best, and learn to remember that you did the same. It may take some time, but he will learn.

QUEEN   Oh, do you think so?

FREDERICK   I am certain of it. He may be fragile now, and very young, but he is not a fool.

QUEEN   But so sensitive. He's weak and frightened.

FREDERICK   He will change.

QUEEN   You have tried to be a comfort to me this evening. I thank you for it. But my life will come to nothing, after all. My poor children, he will never let them marry into my family in England. My daughter will never be the English queen. I will grow old and fatter than I am now, and die of boredom and senility in this dreadful kingdom. I will never escape. I ask you, sir, what can a woman do? What can we poor women do?

(She goes, moving slowly into darkness. Frederick stares after her. His wooden horse begins to move.)

FREDERICK   Plot and scheme, scheme and plot, just like men.

(The wooden horse moves backward into a very dim light as the shadow of the old man appears again on the screen, riding furiously. As it pounds along silently, we hear the song of a flute, odd accompaniment for such a spectacle. When the shadow vanishes, we see two men standing onstage, listening. One is Fredersdorf, the other the Lieutenant, now as Hans Katte, a young officer and companion to the Prince of Prussia. We hear applause for the flute solo, and then Frederick the Prince bursts onto the stage. He is sixteen years old, pale and vulnerable, a boy with bright, feverish eyes, a dizzying excess of talent, and a wild imagination. He is in a state of great excitement, his violence of expressions, which run quickly from rapture to fear, almost alarming. He wears silk evening clothes, is casually unkempt, looks more like a powdered French poet than a Prussian heir. He carries an engraved wooden flute. Behind them, the wooden horse appears again, with Frederick looking down at them from his saddle. Fredersdorf, Katte, and Prince Frederick move swiftly down to the forestage.)

PRINCE FREDERICK   Truth! The truth, now, both of you! Be honest, now, I mean it! What was it like? Tell me!

KATTE   But do we need to? You heard the applause.

PRINCE FREDERICK   Katte, you imbecile, that's not the truth. Anyone will applaud a prince, not necessarily his music.

Now, listen, I'm serious. You are the only honest compasses I have, you two. What did you think? You first, Fredersdorf.

FREDERSDORF   What can I ever tell you about your music? I thought it was very nice. It made me think about the wind at night. I don't know what else to say.

PRINCE FREDERICK   Katte?

KATTE   I have already told you. It was very beautiful.

PRINCE FREDERICK   Oh, flattery, flattery. If you aren't fooling me, if you really mean what you say, Katte, you'll remember this: How many times did my adagio repeat? Were you listening, really? How many times?

KATTE   Four. Yes, four.

PRINCE FREDERICK   Oh, you do mean what you say, you do! Forgive me!

(He embraces Katte with passion.)

It's my fault that I doubted you. You, too, Fredersdorf. Please forgive me.

KATTE   Stop that. You just composed a beautiful sonata. You ought to be proud of yourself.

PRINCE FREDERICK   *(Violently ecstatic)*   Oh, it's more than that! How can I tell you what it means to have that music come out of me.

(He looks at the flute.)

I would rather spend my life with this frail thing and have that wonderful feeling leap out of me than rule a universe of kingdoms. The language of joy, Katte, the

only one, really. It's a swift flight, and a triumphant return. My God, it's enough just to listen, but when I make it myself, when that music comes from *me*, Katte, Fredersdorf, I want to die with joy. Does that embarrass you? Does that seem so absurd?

KATTE   Not to me.

PRINCE FREDERICK   Fredersdorf?

FREDERSDORF   Yes, I'm afraid it does. But that is because I am one thing and you are another. I can't understand it, really.

PRINCE FREDERICK   Good old Fredersdorf. It's, oh . . . it's desire. That's all. Fredersdorf, there's nothing more wonderful than desire.

FREDERSDORF   And nothing more dangerous.

PRINCE FREDERICK   Oh, I don't care! Pure, simple desire. That's all I am! I am nothing else *but* desire! I am a prince, Fredersdorf, and I know how to sing, and I want to dance and shout and, God help me, my friends, conceive beautiful things.

FREDERSDORF   Then that is what you must do.

KATTE   And so you will. You have already begun.

PRINCE FREDERICK   Yes, yes, but sometimes my desire, it's . . . well, I feel as if it will choke me to death. That powerful, really. Listen, Katte, I have finished my comedy, did I tell you?

KATTE   No. I'm delighted. When can I read it?

PRINCE FREDERICK   Tonight. And then . . . more surprises
. . . there's this! A letter. Looks quite ordinary. Paper,
ink. But observe, please, who wrote it. Look, Fredersdorf!
Read us the signature!

FREDERSDORF   Stop teasing. Is this a good man? I hope so.

PRINCE FREDERICK   *(Laughing)*   Give it to Katte.

KATTE   Wonderful. Wonderful.

PRINCE FREDERICK   Who do you think it is, Fredersdorf?
Come on, guess!

FREDERSDORF   Oh, stop that. Tell me or don't.

PRINCE FREDERICK   Voltaire! Voltaire! Oh, you don't know
who he is. God bless you. He is the greatest writer in the
world, Fredersdorf. He is. Really. And he sends me a
letter and calls me the bright hope of Europe. The hope
of mankind! I'll admit I wrote him first, and laid it on
a bit, but the hope of mankind. My God.

FREDERSDORF   Then he is a good man. You are.

PRINCE FREDERICK   Oh, Fredersdorf, don't say that.

KATTE   But he's right. It's true.

PRINCE FREDERICK   No, that's silly. But I would like to be.
I would.

*(The three stand there quietly for a moment, the two
young men struck into silence by this awesome intrusion
of the future, the older man watching his Prince with love
and confidence.)*

PRINCE FREDERICK   Everything good that I possess, I have
had to steal. My music, my philosophy. I write my poems
by the light of one candle at night, with a bedsheet hung
up to hide the light, so I will not be discovered, and
beaten. All my books are hidden in my cabinet that
swings round into the wall, and looks like a mantel-
piece. What deception and strategy I have practiced,
since I was a child. It has been a strange war, my fight
for pleasure and what I think to be good, but I am win-
ning. When I am king, I will go into battle with a different arsenal than most. I will be another man and a different king from all those who have gone before me. I will.

KATTE   *(Quietly)*   Bravo, your Majesty.

*(The General appears, suddenly. He salutes Frederick
coldly, and the mood is shattered. Frederick is immediately hostile and unsure of himself, fleeing into a petu-
lant arrogance that he cannot sustain.)*

PRINCE FREDERICK   Yes?

GENERAL   Your father, the King of Prussia, is waiting for
you, your Royal Highness.

PRINCE FREDERICK   Is he? Oh, yes. Well, all right. Tell him
I'm coming.

*(The General gives him a hard stare and leaves. Fred-
erick hesitates, cannot quite look at his friends. He takes
a deep breath, starts after the General. He goes a few
steps, falters, turns, holds out one arm.)*

PRINCE FREDERICK   Fredersdorf, Katte, come with me!

*(Blackout. In darkness, we hear loud male voices sing-
ing.)*

Then hurray for the love of a country brave
Hurray for the struggle and the strife
Hurray for the strength of a good right arm
Hurray for this day of our life.

Ride away, with our banners streaming past
Ride away, from disgrace and from shame
Ride away, with the knowledge of duty done
Ride away, to the stern fields of Fame.

*(Then we hear a voice bellowing drill commands, and
hands slapping together in sharp rhythm as the commands are executed. It is very boisterous, and when the
lights come up we are in the King's smoking room, his
"Tobacco Parliament." At center, a long, plain wooden
bench, Frederick William seated at its head, and his
cabinet, the Bishop, the Doctor, the Chancellor, there
with him. The General enters, nods to the King, takes up
the clapping, and sits at the bench. They all clap, watching an enormous giant, in his uniform of the Potsdam
Guard, as he bellows out commands of an intricate manual of arms, and then executes them with his rifle. The
giant has been drilled to perfection, his performance is a
harsh, perfect ballet. He finishes, and they applaud. The
King jumps to his feet, babbling with pleasure. He pounds
the giant on the back, embraces him with a ferocious
glee, like a huge child possessing at last a perfect toy
soldier. The giant salutes, and steps back, takes up a
position of attention. Behind it all, in the dim light,
stands the wooden horse, its rider watching closely.)*

FREDERICK WILLIAM   Wonderful. That is the way *that* should
be done.

*(The King sits, takes a deep drink from a huge glass,
and puffs on a clay pipe. Smoke from pipes swarms about
them, joined by more smoke from a peat brazier set up*

*next to the table. The table is littered with glasses, tank-
ards, tobacco, and ashes. At one side is a fool's chair, a
heavy, straight-backed chair with two large hare's ears
stuck to the top of its back. The King presides over his
nightly, gross, untidy Bacchanalia.)*

FREDERICK WILLIAM   Now, gentlemen, we have a very important artistic event scheduled for this evening . . . but
we need his Royal Highness. Where in hell is Fritz?

PRINCE FREDERICK   Here, your Majesty.

(He has been standing unobserved in the background.)

FREDERICK WILLIAM   Come and go when you please, do you?
No respect for my schedule? Who's that with you?

PRINCE FREDERICK   My valet, Fredersdorf. My friend, Lieutenant Hans Katte. I ask your Majesty to allow them
to attend me this evening.

FREDERICK WILLIAM   Attendants, is it? Very well. Your father is always ready to show proper respect, which is a
damn sight more than he gets from you.

(To the General)

Tell them they may *stand* attendant upon his Royal
Highness, and escort his Royal Highness to his chair.

*(The General escorts Frederick to the straight-backed
fool's chair with the hare's ears stuck on it. He blushes
when he sees it, but sits. He stays erect, on the edge of his
seat, while Fredersdorf and Katte move quickly at the
General's gesture, and stand behind him. There is an embarrassed pause, the company uneasy, not wanting to
offend either the present or the future king. Frederick William sees it, and scowls.)*

FREDERICK WILLIAM   All right, now that we're all together, where is that painter? And somebody give his Royal Highness something to drink, to get the starch out of him.

(A large tankard of beer is handed to the Prince, who takes it with disdain.)

FREDERICK WILLIAM   A toast to his Royal Highness. Drink it down, monkey.

(The cabinet echoes the toast with loud voices.)

FREDERICK WILLIAM   Not so quick. Not so quick, gentlemen. Don't fall down on the floor. He's not the king yet. If he keeps prancing about the way he has, he never will be! All, Prince, drink it all!

(The Prince, with a struggle, downs his drink. Frederick William motions, and another is brought to him.)

FREDERICK WILLIAM   Now, then. In honor of his Royal Highness, where's our famous artist! Latest opus! Right now!

(From a group of men standing attendance, the Painter emerges, doing his best to hide his abject servility.)

PAINTER   Your Majesty.

FREDERICK WILLIAM   All right, let's see it. I hope you did your duty.

PAINTER   To the best of my ability, your Majesty. Here it is.

(On the screen appears an oil portrait, a vivid painting of the head and shoulders of a monkey, dressed in a fan-

tastically elaborated uniform, holding a book, wearing glasses, and gesturing as if giving a lecture. They all twist about and look up at it, and as the King laughs, they explode with hilarity. The painting stares out at us.)

FREDERICK WILLIAM   Bravo! Bravo! Now, that's good work! Very sensitive. Fritz, our artist is to be congratulated, don't you think so?

PRINCE FREDERICK   *(Softly)*   Yes, your Majesty.

(He drinks.)

(The cabinet tenders the Painter fulsome and sadistic congratulations. The Painter nods and bows. Frederick William smiles, and drinks.)

PAINTER   Thank you, gentlemen. I am deeply gratified that my efforts have met with his Majesty's approval.

FREDERICK WILLIAM   Approval? Who said I approved anything? Careful what you dare put into the mouth of the King!

PAINTER   Forgive me, your Majesty.

FREDERICK WILLIAM   Overlooked. Artists always make fools of themselves. They can't help it. I never saw one yet who ever said the proper thing. Did you, gentlemen?

(A chorus of No's)

FREDERICK WILLIAM   Did you, Fritz?

PRINCE FREDERICK   No, your Majesty.

FREDERICK WILLIAM   But to be fair, it is a capable work. Decent bright colors and solid brushwork. And I see I have taught you how to paint a Prussian uniform correctly. And at last you were given a subject you could understand!

(Laughter. The Painter bows.)

PAINTER   I am grateful to your Majesty.

FREDERICK WILLIAM   One more thing. As I dab a little paint myself, this is between fellow artists. How did you get your subject to keep still, and hold that fine pose for you? Huh? There's only one answer! It's a self-portrait!

(A roar of laughter. The Painter laughs, too.)

FREDERICK WILLIAM   Well, am I right? Admit it, you scoundrel!

PAINTER   You are right, your Majesty. I confess it.

FREDERICK WILLIAM   All right, that will do. March!

(The Painter leaves, quickly. Frederick William stares at his son.)

FREDERICK WILLIAM   Well, now you can't tell anyone we don't have artistic activity at this court, can you? Can you, Fritz?

PRINCE FREDERICK   No, your Majesty.

FREDERICK WILLIAM   God, he's stiff as a poker! Plays the flute, but can't make honest talk in a roomful of men. Prince, your philosophers and your artists are all fudge and pasty pudding. They make pretty sounds, but more than that is needed to preserve our nation. I'm doing my best to make you see that, son.

PRINCE FREDERICK   I thank your Majesty.

FREDERICK WILLIAM   Your Majesty! Is that the only way you talk to me now?

PRINCE FREDERICK   Forgive me, Papa.

FREDERICK WILLIAM   Here, maybe your fine attendants will learn something from this little school, anyway. You, Fredersdorf, you're an honest man, you served well in the Army. I know that. Watch this little egg. And you, Katte, well, you're too pretty for my taste. I'll be damned if you don't look like a girl. But you can ride a horse. I've seen you. You watch him, too. Agreed?

FREDERSDORF   Yes, your Majesty.

KATTE   Yes, your Majesty.

FREDERICK WILLIAM   Your attendants are satisfactory, Prince. As they will now make reports to me, I'll permit them to attend you closely. Fredersdorf, more to drink for his Royal Highness.

(Fredersdorf takes another tankard to the Prince, who drinks.)

FREDERICK WILLIAM   Don't sip, damn it, drink! Doesn't drink, doesn't hunt. Hides in a thicket and reads a book. At least he doesn't walk on tiptoe any more. Got over that, somehow.

(The members of the cabinet are careful to make their amusement seem affectionate, but they do laugh at the Prince. The Chancellor, who has drunk a good deal himself, crosses the line.)

CHANCELLOR   But, Sire, we must be fair. We all understand he acquitted himself like a man in the harems of the King of Poland, on your recent journey to Dresden.

(Everybody senses danger. You can see them try to draw away from him in their seats. The Chancellor blunders on.)

CHANCELLOR   And there are, so one hears, current and delightful afternoons in Berlin with flutes and a fetching young lady, named Ritter.

FREDERICK WILLIAM   I didn't hear anything about that.

CHANCELLOR   Own up, your Royal Highness! The Presentor's daughter? Duets in the afternoons while her father's away? I know it for a fact. You see, Sire, we have a stirring of the manly instinct, after all!

(He laughs, sees the ugly stare on the King's face, turns pale.)

FREDERICK WILLIAM   Nobody told me. Fritz? Fritz!

PRINCE FREDERICK   Rumors, Papa. To make you angry with me. Rumors.

FREDERICK WILLIAM   We will see. I'll have that Ritter girl examined, Prince. God help her if there's not a smooth plug in that hole. And even if there is, if the little bitch has tried to corrupt you, she'll be whipped in the streets. Will you be debauched into a fool with his brains in his britches?

(To the Chancellor)

And you, sir! Note carefully this is not the court of France! We are not lewd, we do not pander! Such creatures cannot fight; they lose all decency, strength, and honor. We are a poor thing, not elegant, and no diplomat, but we know our honor!

(Drunk, he stands and shouts.)

I contain my lust! In all my long years of marriage, gentlemen, I never once betrayed my vows!

(He strikes the table a tremendous blow.)

Never once! Show me another king in Europe who can say that!

(He sits, flushed, while the cabinet gives praise. Prince Frederick is livid with disgust. Frederick William takes a deep drink and spills beer down his chin onto his chest. He looks up to see his son's expression and stare. His eyelids droop, his voice becomes sluggish, brutal, and dangerous. Slowly)

What are *you* looking at?

(The Prince puts down his tankard and stands up.)

PRINCE FREDERICK   *(Quietly)*   I shall look where I please.

(Panic. Frederick William just stares at him, his mouth working. The cabinet is terrified.)

FREDERICK WILLIAM   *(Hoarsely)*   What? What did he say?

GENERAL   Nothing. Nothing at all, your Majesty.

FREDERICK WILLIAM   What did he say!

PRINCE FREDERICK   *(Ashen)*   I shall look where I please.

BISHOP   The Prince is drunk, Sire, and not responsible for what he says.

DOCTOR A little tipsy, Sire, that's all. It was nothing.

(The King lurches to his feet, spilling beer, dropping his pipe. He is a monstrous figure of drunken, helpless rage. He chokes, and gasps for breath, assaulted from within by his own fury.)

FREDERICK WILLIAM You fop, you God-damned little girl. Monkey, baboon!

(He staggers out from behind the table and moves toward the Prince.)

PRINCE FREDERICK I will look where I please! But I *do* love you. I love you, your Majesty!

(The General moves quickly to the King, on the pretext of helping him stand, but trying to hold him back from the Prince.)

BISHOP There, Sire. Did you hear that? Bravo, Prince.

PRINCE FREDERICK You believe any lie about me anyone tells you, so you can despise me.

(He points to the giant.)

For not being that. Because I'm not that thing!! I don't hate you for it.

(Weeping)

I love you. Papa, you drunken fool. I love you!

GENERAL There, your Majesty. Your son loves his father. A fine boy, a wonderful young man.

FREDERICK WILLIAM What's he saying now?

BISHOP   The Prince just said that although the King has forced him to drink too much, he loves him deeply. Deeply.

FREDERICK WILLIAM   Pretending. Always pretending.

CHANCELLOR   On my word of honor, he is drunk, Sire. See, I just pinched him and he didn't feel a thing.

FREDERICK WILLIAM   He's sly, like a woman. Go to bed, Prince. Somebody put the fool to bed. My God, look at him. Before I'd have let *my* father treat *me* like this, I'd have blown out my brains. Put him to bed!!

(He chokes and coughs violently. Prince Frederick takes a few steps toward him, and holds out his hand.)

PRINCE FREDERICK   Your hand, Papa.

(Frederick William slowly holds it out. Prince Frederick takes it, kisses it, then suddenly falls on his knees, embracing the boots of the King with all the passion of a lover. Sobbing)

PRINCE FREDERICK   Lies, lies, lies, lies! I love and adore you!

(The members of the cabinet praise this spectacle. Frederick William raises his great hands and pets the heaving shoulders of his son.)

FREDERICK WILLIAM   All right. Good. Good!

(He looks around with bleary eyes.)

You see. He is a man of honor. You see?

(Approval from the cabinet. Frederick William keeps patting his son on the back and shoulders, but these

*caresses become harder and stronger. Finally, they fall
upon the boy as open blows.)*

FREDERICK WILLIAM   Listen to me, Fritz. Be open with your
father. Straightforward, aboveboard. No foppishness. Be
a man. Keep your head clear, remember that! Don't let
them cheat you. Always watch the Treasury, don't let
them beggar you! Keep the Army strong! Guns and
hard troops, soldiers who know how to fight. And a sound
economy! Don't let them fool you! Strong, be strong!

*(His fists now are clenched. The blows fall in a manic
rhythm. Murderously, he beats his son.)*

Strong! Strong! Strong! Strong!

*(The Prince reels away, battered, and falls to the floor.
He tries to get up, slips, and sprawls. Fredersdorf and
Katte come to him. He cannot look at them. They help
him to his feet and walk him out of the room. Frederick
William stumbles back to the head of his table.)*

FREDERICK WILLIAM   To his mother. Now everyone will
think I have treated my son badly. I suppose they will
have a low opinion of me.

*(He glares about, stands weaving, enclosed in a sullen,
maudlin dignity.)*

Well, that's all right. So do I.

*(He stares about with unfocused eyes. His rage returns.
He lifts his arms and brings his fists down on the table.
He begins to smash everything within reach. The lights
go out on him, but the painted monkey on the screen
still stares out at us. Then it fades.*
*Drums, in short military staccato bursts. The stage is
cleared, and Frederick's horse moves downstage. Prince
Frederick, with a scarlet cloak over his shoulders, comes*

out into a dim light on the forestage. Fredersdorf is with him, and hands him a small traveling bag.)

PRINCE FREDERICK   Thanks. Now get away from here, Fredersdorf.

FREDERSDORF   You have never insulted me before. Why do you do it now? You must take me with you. What am I without you?

PRINCE FREDERICK   For the last time, no. I don't know what's going to happen when I get to England; neither does anybody else. You wouldn't be safe, and that settles that. Hurry now. Good-by.

FREDERSDORF   No. I will never desert you.

PRINCE FREDERICK   It's an order, old man.

(Fredersdorf blinks, nods. He reaches out to embrace Frederick, who steps back. Fredersdorf grabs him, embraces him roughly, leaves. Frederick the Prince stares after him for a moment, then looks about, paces nervously. Behind him, the black shadow of Frederick the King looms above him; light falls on his ravaged face. The Prince wheels about suddenly.)

PRINCE FREDERICK   Yes? Who is it?

KING FREDERICK   Good evening. You are out very late, your Royal Highness.

PRINCE FREDERICK   What of that?

KING FREDERICK   Well, it is a bit unusual to find the Crown Prince strolling about alone at one end of the kingdom, in the middle of the night.

PRINCE FREDERICK   And who are you, sir?

KING FREDERICK   Let us say I am an officer in your father's army.

PRINCE FREDERICK   Then mind your behavior. It's a **nice** evening, and I wish to enjoy it. Alone.

KING FREDERICK   Not quite alone. A few hopes, I think, keep you company. You see a new world just over the French border. All your youth is coiled like a spring, to catapult you into it. A fresh world, a new universe.

PRINCE FREDERICK   You're very perceptive, and rather ominous. I don't care for your company at all.

KING FREDERICK   That is not surprising. It is quite natural that you should find me unpleasant.

PRINCE FREDERICK   Then take yourself off!

KING FREDERICK   That is not so easy, your Royal Highness.

PRINCE FREDERICK   I am giving you an order!

KING FREDERICK   That cannot be obeyed. It is impossible, my youth.

PRINCE FREDERICK   At once! Do you hear me, at once!

KING FREDERICK   No use. At this moment, the Prince loses.

PRINCE FREDERICK   What?

KING FREDERICK   Be so good as to turn around.

(From the shadows the Chancellor emerges.)

CHANCELLOR   Good evening, your Royal Highness. I regret
to say that your adventure is over. Your plot was discovered several days ago, I'm afraid. Hans Katte is
already in prison. He will not join you here tonight.

PRINCE FREDERICK   What are you talking about?

CHANCELLOR   Your letters were very carelessly sent. They
were easily intercepted, read, and passed on. There will
be no horses, no Hans Katte, and no daring night gallop
over the French border. Your father has known for days
that you and Katte, desperate children, were deserting
the kingdom together.

PRINCE FREDERICK   Ridiculous!

KING FREDERICK   Is it? Another minute and you will be
under arrest. Listen! Can you hear the click of the
boots?

PRINCE FREDERICK   Oh, God, it's true. Get me a horse!

KING FREDERICK   Too late.

*(The General and several soldiers appear. They all salute
the Prince.)*

GENERAL   I deeply regret to inform your Royal Highness
that you are from this moment under arrest. If you re-
sist, our orders from his Majesty state we must shoot
to kill.

CHANCELLOR   Please respect us. We must do our duty.

(The Prince looks at them with disgust.)

PRINCE FREDERICK   Do you think I don't understand that?

(He stares out. The figure on the horse lifts his head.)

What will happen to me?

(As the Prince is marched off, the wooden horse moves forward, carrying Frederick the King, rigid in his saddle.)

VOICE OF KING FREDERICK   In a fashion, my youth, you will survive. You will be taken to prison. You will not beg, at first.

(Around him and his great horse now resound the voices of his past.)

VOICE OF FREDERICK WILLIAM   Why were you a traitor? Why did you desert?

VOICE OF PRINCE FREDERICK   Because you treat me like a slave, not a son.

VOICE OF FREDERICK WILLIAM   You have betrayed your father, as well as your country.

VOICE OF THE QUEEN   Your Majesty! Your Majesty!

VOICE OF FREDERICK WILLIAM   Stop wringing your hands. Your worthless son will soon be dead and trouble you no more.

VOICE OF THE QUEEN   O God in heaven, you are monster enough to kill him?

VOICE OF FREDERICK WILLIAM   The penalty for treason in Prussia is death.

(Drums, the bursts coming closer and closer together. The wooden horse moves back, and the light fades except for a slight wash on the face of Frederick the King.

Lights come up on a platform, where Frederick the Prince stands dressed in a brown, sacklike prison gown. The Bishop is with him.)

BISHOP   Compose yourself, your Royal Highness. Everything that lives must die; it is the will of God. Submit yourself, and pray for your kingdom, for your father, and for your immortal soul.

PRINCE FREDERICK   *(Wildly)*   But I'm his son! I am the Prince! He won't kill me, he can't! He wouldn't dare!

VOICE OF THE GENERAL   Your Majesty, Lieutenant Hans Katte has been found guilty of desertion. This court-martial has sentenced him to life imprisonment. However, this court cannot render verdict upon the Crown Prince. That judgment must lie solely in the hands of your Majesty, the King.

VOICE OF FREDERICK WILLIAM   So be it. Give me those papers.

PRINCE FREDERICK   Impossible! He will never do that. My mother, the King of England, all of Europe will protect me!

BISHOP   He is the king. He can do what he likes, my son. But his rule does not extend to heaven, and this he knows. He has composed this prayer for you to recite, to petition Almighty God for forgiveness. Will you receive it?

PRINCE FREDERICK   No! No! I don't believe it!

(Drums, steadily. An executioner in a black mask carries a chopping block onto the stage and sets it down. He stands with his ax in his hands. Frederick stares at him. The General appears on the platform.)

GENERAL   I have come to do my duty, your Royal Highness. Please respect me.

PRINCE FREDERICK   It's not possible! Papa! Papa!

(The drums reach a crescendo and stop. Silence. The King leans forward on his wooden horse.)

KING FREDERICK   Now you will beg.

(A figure walks out of the darkness, wearing a hat that shadows his face, dressed in the same brown prison gown as Frederick, looking just like him. Soldiers march beside him. The figure moves to the executioner's chopping block, turns, and looks up at Frederick.)

PRINCE FREDERICK   Katte! Katte! In heaven's name, no! Oh Katte, for God's sake, forgive me!

(Katte removes his hat, attempting a gallant, sweeping bow of youthful bravado. He tries to bow smoothly, but he is shaking very badly, and his courage is coming to pieces.)

KATTE   It is nothing. May you achieve all your dreams. I am happy to die for so fine a prince.

PRINCE FREDERICK   *(Turning away)*   Oh, no. No.

GENERAL   The verdict of life imprisonment against Lieutenant Hans Katte is personally countermanded by the King of Prussia. Lieutenant Hans Katte, immoral corruptor of the Prince of Prussia, is sentenced to death by decapitation. This execution will take place immediately, under the following condition:

(He takes the Prince by the shoulders.)

Please respect me, your Royal Highness.

(He turns him about, facing the execution.)

Your father decrees that you must watch.

(Drums again. Katte drops his hat, removes his gown, opens the collar of his shirt. He crosses himself, mutters "Lord Jesus," and then kneels, placing his neck upon the block.)

PRINCE FREDERICK   Katte! Katte! Katte! Katte!

(The drums stop. The executioner raises his ax. On his horse, his body twisted by the ravages of these memories, King Frederick stands in his stirrups and swings his bright sword up above his head. The executioner comes down with the ax. Blackout.

  The Prince screams in the darkness: a long, full, youthful cry of terror that merges into another cry by the same voice, but old now and hoarse and sorrowful. Light falls on the King riding his wooden horse, waving his sword, then throwing it away from him, screaming.

  The drums take up the canter rhythm. The shadow of the King on his horse appears on the screen, galloping furiously. Frederick the Great gathers his long reins and beats his horse on both flanks.)

FREDERICK   Faster!

(He lashes his inert, wooden horse.)

Faster!

Act 2
The King

(During the intermission, one of Frederick's flute concertos or sonatas is played. On the last note of the flute, we proceed into darkness, and hear the sounds of wind and rain. Low thunder. A flash of lightning. We see the two soldiers sent riding ahead from the battlefield. They stand writhing with anxiety.)

SOLDIER 1   But he won't do it, for God's sake! Leave a battlefield? He'd never do that. He won't come.

SOLDIER 2   Oh, yes, he will. And he'll kill us. Murder us both.

SOLDIER 1   But it isn't our fault! We didn't do it.

SOLDIER 2   He won't care. He'll kill us all.

SOLDIER 1   Maybe the rain stopped him. Christ, he's seventy-three years old, after all.

SOLDIER 2   At his reviews last year I watched him ride in the rain for six hours. He'll come galloping over that hill right there before you know where you are. No, there's only one thing to do. We don't have any choice.

SOLDIER 1   What?

SOLDIER 2   Dig it up again.

SOLDIER 1   Ah, no, that's disgusting. I won't do that!

SOLDIER 2   Then maybe you would rather tell the King, who left a battlefield and rode all night in the rain, that nobody thought he was coming, so the body is already buried under six feet of dirt. Yes?

SOLDIER 1   Ah, but my God, the thing isn't even human! It's revolting!

SOLDIER 2   Come on! Let's find some lieutenant to give us permission to dig it up. Hurry, it's all we can do.

SOLDIER 1   All right. Let's find an officer. Horrible! God damn it, it's revolting!

(They run off. Thunder and wind. On the screens, Frederick rides his horse homeward through the storm and the memories of his life. The wooden horse appears in semidarkness at one side of the stage at the rear. On the horse perches the black shadow of Frederick, overlooking the stage. This is now a double, whose dark figure will overlook the action.

Bells, deep and mournful. A church organ plays funeral music. The storm vanishes, and with it the rider on the screen. There now we see the self-portrait of Frederick William again, but with a large black band swathed diagonally across it.

Each thinking separate thoughts, the Prussian cabinet walks onstage, slowly, one by one, coming from different directions. They acknowledge each other with a nod, move away, and stand waiting, as if attending the formal procedures of a ritual's end, just before settling down to business. They glance at each other from time to time, uneasily. The funeral music ends. The General and the Chancellor maneuver themselves so that they are standing side by side. They speak with studied casualness, in low voices.)

GENERAL   Over, thank heaven. A battle plan, you know, is simplicity itself compared to a state funeral.

CHANCELLOR   It was flawless. Magnificent. Congratulations.

GENERAL   Thank you. I thought the shrouded throne was a nice touch. And I had hoped that our new monarch, with all his taste for luxury and dramatics, would have sat there and preened in the public eye. But no, he sat in the congregation and pretended to cry, like everyone else.

CHANCELLOR   Whims. We may expect many. For instance, and I'm not exactly sure I should be the one to tell you this, but only an hour ago I received some instructions about the finances of the Royal Guard. His father's giants, I mean. But of course, you knew about it some time ago.

GENERAL   I beg your pardon?

CHANCELLOR   Yes, I wondered if you'd been told.

GENERAL   Told what, please?

CHANCELLOR   They're junked. No more money for them. Dismissed, today. The roads of Prussia at this moment hold several hundred bewildered giants, seven feet tall, wandering about wondering what to do with themselves. It does seem like you would have been informed.

GENERAL   Deliberate, silly gesture. I won't be surprised if he commands every soldier to carry a flute instead of a rifle and march past the reviewing stand on tiptoe. Playing French music. Skipping off to battle maneuvers under a dancing master.

CHANCELLOR   Delightful notion, but is it so funny, after all? He is the King, don't you understand? It's true, impossible as it may seem to . . .

(Takes in the Doctor)

all of us.

DOCTOR   *(Who has quietly approached them)*   What kind of king, then, do you make out of a French fop?

CHANCELLOR   That will depend on us. On our skill.

GENERAL   Exactly. Just how skillful are we, these days?

CHANCELLOR   *(Smiling at the Doctor)*   Let's find out.

(They become a trio.)

Perhaps we might discuss the health of the King. But frankly, you understand.

DOCTOR   I understand. I am glad to see you concerned about it.

GENERAL   Oh, come now. Our Minister of Finance did say frankly. If you prefer evasion, I hope it will make you happy when physicians arrive from Paris to take your pulse—and your position.

DOCTOR   *(Decides)*   All right. He won't last a year.

CHANCELLOR   Really?

(All ears prick up. The Bishop begins to drift over. When the Doctor finishes, they are all standing together.)

DOCTOR   Really. Our monarch is the ruins of a twenty-nine-year nervous disaster. A hanging garden of uprooted nerves. He sweats through three bedsheets every night, exhausted and sleepless. When he does drift off, violent nightmares. And for the past ten years, well, he has slaved like a common clerk to keep his father from disowning him. Drills himself like a hussar, does everything he hates and despises. And then all that scribbling, at night mostly, and those hysterical flute concerts, for which he practices four hours a day, always in deadly fear his father will find out about them. And, of course, his marriage . . . well . . .

(They all smile and shrug.)

DOCTOR Do you know that four years after the marriage that wretched woman still primps and waits for him every night? Pitiful.

GENERAL Pity them both. That little frump is quite enough to turn anyone's stomach. His father's final blow—marrying him to a Hausfrau.

CHANCELLOR But his stomach would be turned in any case, were she the most ravishing woman in Europe. Does he still flaunt those page boys?

DOCTOR He drops a kerchief now and then. The boy who picks it up understands he will come in for breakfast the following morning.

GENERAL Breakfast? Disgusting.

CHANCELLOR Isn't it possible . . . ?

DOCTOR I tried. Not one of those little darlings had a word to say. They were all positively embarrassed.

CHANCELLOR Embarrassed? Them?

DOCTOR   Well, you see, the rumor goes that he is quite pas-
sive, and it's the page boy who does the screwing. But it
must upset them to talk about it, or something. Anyway,
they either worship him or are scared to death or both.
Perhaps they even like him. Who can tell? They admit
nothing more than helping him dress and sharing his
morning pot of chocolate.

GENERAL   Ridiculous!

BISHOP   Yes, it really is, isn't it?

*(They all turn to stare at the Bishop. Then they recognize
his presence, and nod gravely.)*

BISHOP   But at least there is no question of an heir. Not
his, I mean, God be praised. That's something to consider.

GENERAL   But how? He is the king today, this minute. We
never quite seem to get that through our heads. And we
do *not* need sermons on his conception of the Supreme
Being.

BISHOP   His idea of God is not very elevated. God is the
way everything works, that's all. And I will be very
amused to see what happens to the Treasury when this
philosophical hedonist gets his hands on it, as he will today.

CHANCELLOR   Not very skillful, are we?

GENERAL   No. Gentlemen, let us bury these bristling rival-
ries. Our nation is in peril. Prussia has inherited God
knows what for a king. And if he doesn't fall apart by
himself, the large fish that swim about our borders will
gobble him and us within a year. We must face our

plain duty. It is up to us whether this nation shall endure or perish.

DOCTOR   That's very inspiring. However, we must learn to trust each other first. You'll admit it's a slight obstacle.

CHANCELLOR   But there is no reason why he should frighten us any more as a king than he did as a prince. We know what he is: a frightened little pervert who wallows in sensual pleasure to escape the burdens of his existence. It isn't unusual in kings, after all. We only have to agree among ourselves which way we pull him by the nose. Otherwise, along with being eaten alive by the rest of Europe, we'll die of boredom at concerts and poetry readings.

BISHOP   I deplore your harshness. But not your logic.

GENERAL   Army, Church, Government, Science. I think we are each of us familiar, to say the least, with the ambitions of the other. Well, do we fight among ourselves, or do we march together, for the preservation of our land?

DOCTOR   We fight among ourselves. But sensibly, which means we let each other know what we are telling the King.

BISHOP   Gross expression, but accurate logic. Now, how much *do* we tell the King?

CHANCELLOR   As little as possible.

ALL   Agreed!

(Fredersdorf enters.)

FREDERSDORF   The King.

(Frederick enters. He is now about thirty, but looks much older. Ten years have passed since Katte's execution. Until this moment, he has subjugated himself completely to his father's will. He carries his flute.)

FREDERICK   Well, gentlemen, my congratulations on the funeral. He might have preferred something less elaborate, but he had no choice, did he? And now the people think they loved him all the time, and it was very moving. Tomorrow morning I want to see all the accounts of that spectacle, down to the last penny. That was a lot of velvet drapery you had hanging about. If anyone made a killing on it, I warn you the accounts will not be passed. As for that . . .

(He swings around to look up at his father's portrait above them.)

Who measured him?

DOCTOR   I did, your Majesty, as you commanded.

FREDERICK   And?

DOCTOR   At death, your father's body measured eight feet six inches around the stomach.

FREDERICK   Really? That much?

DOCTOR   I measured him myself, Sire.

FREDERICK   You win, Fredersdorf. I was off by two feet. Gentlemen, with that we will pass over the domestic torments of this great Prince. He was an excellent administrator. He was an honest man, who worked hard for his people. He was my father, and I loved him. But now he is gone. Remove the portrait.

(The portrait fades from the screen. Pesne's charming, idealized portrait of Frederick as a young man appears.)

FREDERICK   Vivid? Lovely? Well, we will see. Now, then, period of mourning, one month. During which time we all have a lot of work to do. At the conclusion of that time, a celebration here, a fete, if you please, à la française. I am composing a concerto for flute and orchestra for the occasion. I have drawn up certain recommendations and procedures for each of you to consult and follow. I expect you to sweat just as much over your offices as I do over my music. Fredersdorf.

(Fredersdorf nods and leaves. Frederick plays a quick arpeggio on his flute.)

FREDERICK   In the meantime, I invite each of you, in turn, to dine with me, alone. Great men, such as yourselves, must be considered singly. One at a time, as you deserve. All together you tend to distract, each one from the other. . . .

(Another arpeggio)

Like children. Don't frown, General, I won't disband the Army. Hardly. Nor will the Church suffer, exactly, nor the Treasury, nor the Royal Academies. And you have all been granted certain special positions and advantages, which you will be told about in good time.

(A quick scale, as Fredersdorf comes in, loaded down with a mountainous stack of papers and documents. The cabinet, seeing this, buzzes among itself, in protest at this treatment. Frederick plays a delicate little trill on the flute, lingering on the last note until they are quiet.)

FREDERICK   But, gentlemen, we must face the fact that my
father left me a Prussian monarchy that is, if I may be
permitted the expression, a kind of hermaphrodite. Neither one thing nor the other, if you follow me. Not quite
a kingdom, but a little bit more than an electorate. So
here we are, while a very interested and amorous Europe
is at our window, waiting to see just what kind of sexual
organs we intend to display. Gentlemen, at such a dramatic moment, can you afford to disappoint? I am delighted to see that each of you looks so eager for the
tasks that lie ahead of you. As for me, well, this afternoon I must write to the King of France, compose a largo,
make up a poem for Voltaire, and alter the constitution
of the Army. Fredersdorf has your instructions. Good
morning.

*(He turns on his heel, picks up his music, which Freders-
dorf holds out for him, and leaves. Simultaneously, we
hear the opening chords of Frederick's C-Major Concerto for Flute and Orchestra. The flamboyant first move-
ment plays from this point to its conclusion. The cabinet members, stunned, receive great piles of instructions
from Fredersdorf, and, bewildered, they move off in different directions. The music swells. From above, celebration banners, chandeliers, royal trappings. The brilliant portrait of Frederick as a young prince remains.
The introduction of the orchestra now leads to the first
notes of the flutist. Frederick appears in a bright light,
strikes a professional stance, and breathes into his flute.
He plays with swift sureness, moving his head and his
body in total command of his music. The rhapsodic but
militant flights of the flute fill the theater. When the
orchestra responds again, the members of the cabinet,
like puppets on strings, step into various downlights, and
proclaim the decrees of the King, and the music fades
under so they can be heard, rises again when they finish. As he plays, Frederick watches them, and like the*

Pied Piper, never loses his beat. If it is possible for a flutist to smile as he plays, Frederick does.)

DOCTOR   The King of Prussia announces the European publication of his book, the *Anti-Machiavel*. This work, prepared by the young Prince in preparation for his reign, edited and presented to the world by M. Voltaire, of France, is the open refutation of the doctrines of Machiavelli, who would rule by deceit. These moral axioms and political vows declare that a king is only the first servant of his people, and they proclaim to the four corners of the earth this ascension of a philosopher to a throne.

(Frederick plays.)

GENERAL   His Majesty announces the abolition of physical torture. No citizen will ever be threatened by it again. All courts are informed that his Majesty requires his own review of all decisions of imprisonment, no matter how slight. Like the King, judges will serve, not punish, the people.

(Frederick plays.)

CHANCELLOR   Taxes are reduced, embargoes lifted, relief projects ordained, school systems commanded, the hunting privileges of the nobility abolished. Petitioners may come to the King at any time. They will be heard.

(Frederick plays.)

BISHOP   Every man in Prussia is at liberty to find his own way up to heaven. Go to church, any kind of church you please, or stay at home and sleep, as you wish.

(Frederick plays, his motion and attack more and more fierce, as if in the sweat of his body and the flight of his

music, he is creating his kingdom. The cabinet shifts about, moving very fast, receives more instructions, and reads again, this time all of them very tired.)

BISHOP *(Hoarsely)* The King declares complete freedom of the Prussian newspapers. A newspaper must be free, you know, simply to be interesting.

CHANCELLOR *(Dismayed)* There is a new Academy of Science and Art. A new opera house is being built. A Royal Gazette, in French, has been subsidized by the King. He will be a frequent contributor.

GENERAL *(Sweating)* The King orders the creation of sixteen new battalions within the month. A new manual of Prussian drill will be issued tomorrow from his own hand. To all commanders, however, this notice: military arrogance will be severely punished. Any officer whose command is responsible for harshness or disrespect toward private citizens will be court-martialed within the hour.

DOCTOR *(Fiercely)* To the masters of darkness, superstition, and oppression, this young Monarch offers swift destruction if they approach his kingdom. But to all enlightened spirits of modern Europe, in this age of reason, Frederick II, King in Prussia, offers his welcome, his protection, and the liberty to work with him for the advancement of humanity. Long may he reign!

(The cabinet now stands below Frederick, in a circle radiating from him. They kneel as he brings his concerto to a close with ringing authority. Frederick moves downstage, mopping his face, and pressing his hand to his side. He grits his teeth in pain and catches his breath. Fredersdorf comes down behind him.)

FREDERSDORF See, see, now you're trembling. All those spices for dinner and then playing right afterward. You get too excited. See, bad color. Liverish. How are your hemorrhoids?

FREDERICK All right. How are yours?

FREDERSDORF Terrible. Stomach cramps?

FREDERICK *(Catching his breath)* Yes, yes. It takes more trouble to manage this wretched body of mine than fifteen kingdoms. I will try that new purge of yours. Double strength, if you please. Do you need some, too?

FREDERSDORF *(Smiling)* Yes.

FREDERICK Fine. We will suffer together.

(Fredersdorf leaves as the messenger comes in, bringing a letter. On the screens, hands passing letters back and forth. Frederick beams with pleasure and opens the letter. Upstage, in a bright light, we see a small, skeletal little man in his sixties, leaning on a cane: Voltaire. He is very ugly and very elegant, and his carbuncle eyes glitter.)

VOLTAIRE A young prince once wrote to an ancient scribbler, and sent him an "Ode Against Flattery." This doubtful old man of letters thought then that a prince writing odes against flattery was as strange as a pope composing hymns against immaculate conceptions. However, they became friends. They published a book together, condemning Machiavelli. But the cynical old historian reflected that the first thing true pupils of Machiavelli do is write books against him. Still, he could not help being filled with hope. Was it possible that here could be the philosopher-prince of whom poor Plato dreamed, and here a weathered poet to guide him? Miracle of miracles, the Prince survives, to become the King who will defend Europe against tyranny and superstition. With all my heart I salute our Solomon of the North.

FREDERICK   Perhaps Don Quixote rather than Solomon, but we will see. At any rate, it was to you the Prince said all his prayers. He knelt by his bed and prayed to his saint: the greatest writer in the world and the only fearless man in Europe, Voltaire. And now, my Deity, are you pleased with the literary apprentice who has loved you?

VOLTAIRE   For one phrase alone—the king is the first servant of the people—will I sing his praises until the day I die.

(Frederick laughs. The tone of his voice changes and he smiles wryly.)

FREDERICK   I admit it has a certain ring. But we are philosopher-poets, you and I, and we will not be deceived, not even by ourselves. For the people make up a rabble, and the rabble makes up the State, the king is the first servant of that State, and all good dogs may rely on me.

(A soldier quickly brings Frederick a letter, which he reads swiftly while Voltaire is talking.)

VOLTAIRE   *(Chuckling)*   Most kings are frightened to death to hear the truth, yet you undertake to teach it.

FREDERICK   No, no, it is you who must teach. You must keep faith with the Prince by instructing the King, as always.

VOLTAIRE   Then let me say only this: from such a dazzling pinnacle, I do apprehend you may at last be in danger of conceiving too great a contempt for shivering mankind. I will blot this out and be corrected when I know you have not succumbed to that final plague of kings.

FREDERICK   I have suffered so much from that disease in others, I do not think it will infect me now. And the greatest of writers, after all, sometimes contract that little malady themselves.

VOLTAIRE   The only difference between the maladies of kings and of writers is that the latter are more ridiculous. Rule your Prussian kingdom, your Majesty. Voltaire with all of Europe stands amazed at your brilliance.

FREDERICK   But when are you coming to live with me? You will stand officially among my titles: Frederick, King of Prussia, Prince Elector of Brandenburg, and Possessor of Voltaire! I will give you the greatest royal welcome any citizen has ever received.

VOLTAIRE   That would make an old man very happy. But other friendships hold me here and will not let me leave. You were always more a man to me than a prince, and you will, without doubt, permit me, my Lord, to prefer my friends even to kings.

(He bows, and the light goes out on him.)

FREDERICK   *(Smiling quietly)*   All in good time. All in good time.

(He folds the letter he has been holding, places it in a coat pocket. He breathes into his flute. The cabinet comes bustling on, very energetic and pleased with themselves. They have recovered from their reversals, and have set

sail on their new course as faithful ministers to a high morality.)

CHANCELLOR   Your Majesty, we hasten to inform you of the death of the Austrian Emperor.

DOCTOR   The Holy Roman Empire of the German Nation must now be led by his only heir, the twenty-three-year-old daughter. It is a ticklish moment, Sire.

BISHOP   Peace in Europe depends upon swift support of Maria Theresa's rightful claim to her throne. Your Majesty is aware that every shark in the water waits to see her claim challenged. What is worse, the lady is in delicate health. Quite pregnant, alas, and cannot endure a coronation for some time.

GENERAL   To support your Majesty's recent declarations of loyalty to the Empire, I propose maneuvers to strengthen both borderlands.

BISHOP   I propose divine services, imploring God to bless this union of Austria and Prussia.

CHANCELLOR   I propose further endorsement of all your Majesty's treaties with Austria, to publicly demonstrate your loyalty to your sworn word.

DOCTOR   And I propose a mutual congress of artistic and scientific intercourse. Its theme: Peace!

CHANCELLOR   Shall we place these suggestions into concrete form, Sire? It would be well to make yourself heard at once. The world awaits the first firm action of the philosopher-King.

(They all stare at him, waiting. He is smiling faintly and staring out blankly into space. They look at each

*other and then they become aware that he is tapping
his flute now against his boot, quite as if it is an officer's
military baton. He does not answer them.)*

CHANCELLOR   Shall we continue, your Majesty?

FREDERICK   No.

*(He points suddenly to the Lieutenant, who has been
standing in the background.)*

Who is that young officer there?

GENERAL   *(Surprised)*   My aide, Sire. Lieutenant Kort.

FREDERICK   *(Quickly)*   What name?

LIEUTENANT   *(He steps forward.)*   Kort, your Majesty.

FREDERICK   *(Gazing at him and smiling. They stand facing
each other, recalling the positions of the Prince and Hans
Katte.)*   Well, then, Lieutenant. What do you think
about it?

LIEUTENANT   Your Majesty, I cannot say. I am a very young
and inexperienced officer.

FREDERICK   Quite right. A child, in fact. What happens to
children, Lieutenant?

LIEUTENANT   They change, Sire. They grow.

FREDERICK   Larger, in fact. And how does the child feel
then?

LIEUTENANT   Better. Bigger. Resolved.

FREDERICK   Perfect. And what then?

LIEUTENANT   He must continue to grow. The child must improve himself. Do more.

FREDERICK   Gentlemen, the first stern law of life, for nations as for children, as this handsome baby so clearly sees, is growth. Enlargement, if you will.

(The members of the cabinet look at each other, very puzzled.)

FREDERICK   The death of the Emperor offers changes in the structure of Europe we must think twice about refusing. I hope none of you has forgotten my father's just claim to twenty thousand square miles of Austria? To all of the Silesian province?

CHANCELLOR   Your Majesty, that disputed claim lies buried in the past! You cannot possibly hope to resurrect it now!

FREDERICK   *(A quick burst of anger, quite ferocious)*   And who will tell me not to? Control yourself when you speak to the King! You may bite your hands tomorrow for what you say today!

GENERAL   Sire, please consider military reality. You will have to fight. Your troops are beautifully drilled, but the men of the vast Austrian Army have all seen the wolf. Your father did create an impressive force on the parade ground, but he was always careful never to take it into the field of battle.

FREDERICK   Because my father's soldiers are handsome, you think them only pretty. Well, General, I am going to show you that a Prussian soldier fights even better than he looks! This month, gentlemen, it is not going to be a question of philosophy, poetry, and music, but gunpowder, trenches, and steel. Arrange yourselves accordingly.

BISHOP   Attack Austria? To invade her now? Such careless levity, Sire, is absolutely unheard of!

FREDERICK   Well, I am trying to be original.

DOCTOR   Can your Majesty be fully aware of the consequences of his proposals? It is hard for us to believe it.

FREDERICK   I am aware of my duty, sir, and the life to which I was born. This little project will bring a reputation to the King and power to the State, both very necessary before peace and music can be maintained.

(He takes the letter received during his scene with Voltaire and waves it at them.)

The orchestration has already been prepared. While the flutes are playing here tonight, I will lead thirty-six battalions and twenty-seven squadrons across the Silesian border, into a defenseless province against a pregnant woman, and I suggest you all be at my side, singing loudly. Lieutenant!

LIEUTENANT   Your Majesty!

FREDERICK   To me!

(They move swiftly upstage, where the Lieutenant helps Frederick into military uniform and hands him a shining sword. A band crashes into the Hohenfriedberg "Victory March." Militant banners, drums, sections of stacked rifles descend from above. Soldiers appear on the screens. The cabinet, still carrying their documents of peace and philosophical friendship, stare aghast. Then they look at each other, take deep breaths, and address us once more.)

BISHOP   With the blessings of Almighty God, the King now searches for justice! In the name of the Father, and of the Son, and of the Holy Ghost.

DOCTOR   Men of Prussia! The King has noticed that we are now surrounded by ladies. Elizabeth in Russia, Maria Theresa in Austria, and Pompadour in the bedroom of the King of France. Follow him now, and impress upon them a new birth of Prussian manhood!

GENERAL   The King of Prussia offers the Queen of Austria the protection of his allies and his Army. In return, he asks for the province of Silesia and he will accept nothing less. If it is not offered to him with good grace, he will take it.

CHANCELLOR   Courage! We have a great king, a good Army, and money in the Treasury. Our cause is just, and our resources prepared!

FREDERICK   *(Taking the stage)*   And besides all that, I want to see my name in the newspapers.

(He raises his sword and gives a battle speech, glancing at the Lieutenant, who stands by him, drunk with worship.)

Prussians! Our fate now lies in the hands of Fortune! All that remains is to fight bravely and do what we can to alter Chance! Farewell! I follow you to the rendezvous of Fame, which now awaits us all!

(Drums. Cannon fire. Smoke pours onto the stage. Through it steps King Frederick, sword in his hand. He comes down to the edge of the forestage and stares up into the sky. His eyes are wet, his words now in absolute earnest.)

FREDERICK   Oh, my great poor fat fool of a father. Today as I rode to battle, I passed a farmhouse. A woman was standing under an apple tree, scolding her little boy, who had climbed up to the topmost branch and would not come down. I stopped to see what was the matter. The boy was three years old. His father was dead, and he had climbed the tree when he was told his father went to heaven, to be just that much closer to him. Am I any different, the King, riding to war? What are you doing up there? Who gets your blows on his back? Do you throw inkpots at the white angels? Is your belly still eight feet six inches fat?

(Great tears roll down his cheeks. Cannons roar in the distance. He holds out his arms, the light catches the blade of his sword.)

What do you think of your little fop who plays the flute? Would *you* take the field against him? And if you could really be in heaven, and I should one day stand before you again, will you promise to be what you were, and, if I conquer the world, strike me just as hard?

(Explosion. Smoke engulfs him, and billows about the stage. The General and the Lieutenant emerge from the smoke. The General throws down his hat and stamps on it.)

GENERAL   God damn it, why didn't he let me attack! We had them in Mollwitz drinking beer and singing songs, God damn it, and now they know where we are! Madman! Lunatic!

LIEUTENANT   *(Frantic)*   The King! The King!

(Frederick enters through the smoke, coolly. He looks at the General's hat, then at the General.)

FREDERICK   You may now attack, if you please.

GENERAL   Why not three hours ago! Three hours, your Majesty!

FREDERICK   I reserve command of this little venture to my-self alone. The world shall not think the King of Prussia marches to war under a tutor. If you can gain sufficient control of yourself, we will proceed.

GENERAL   Your Majesty, in the name of God, put up your sword and let me lead the Army. You will be killed, and everything ended.

FREDERICK   That's stupid. Of course I must lead the Army.

(With his sword, he spears the General's hat.)

Get hold of yourself. You look scared to death.

(To the Lieutenant)

And you, you pretty little thing, get on your horse and fight for your country. General?

(He holds out the hat on the sword. Explosion. Great puffs of smoke engulf them. More explosions, rifle fire, sounds of galloping horses and all the chaos of battle. On the screen, battle etchings. They emerge again from the smoke. Frederick is dazed.)

FREDERICK   What happened? What happened?

GENERAL   It's over, that's what happened. The Austrian cavalry crushed our center. It's hopeless!

FREDERICK   Do you mean to tell me I've lost?

GENERAL   All over, Sire. Full retreat or we will be massacred! Lieutenant, the King's horse!

FREDERICK   Well, Jesus Christ.

LIEUTENANT   This way! This way, your Majesty!

*(Frederick disappears into the smoke. The General
watches him go, then spins around quickly.)*

GENERAL   Now, God damn it, maybe I can get something
done! Major, regroup artillery. Colonel, the infantry out
of the woods. Cavalry and assault on left flanks!

*(He wades into the smoke. Sounds of a horse galloping
furiously. Frederick emerges far downstage, waving anx-
iously to a soldier who appears upstage on a platform,
walking guard duty.)*

FREDERICK   Open the fort! Open the gates! It's the King!

SOLDIER   My ass.

(He fires at the King.)

FREDERICK   God Almighty!

*(He jumps back into the smoke. Explosions and rifle
fire, dying down to a low mutter.)*

GENERAL   Where? Where is he?

LIEUTENANT   In that farmhouse. In the barn. He tried to
get into the garrison last night but some fool shot at him.
He's been holed up in there all night long, thinking he
lost the battle, crying and writing verses.

GENERAL   We would have lost it if I hadn't got rid of
him. Does he know I countered and won?

(Frederick emerges from the smoke.)

FREDERICK   He does.

(With a wry smile)

Congratulations. You are promoted. Decorated. Savior of Prussia, you have rescued the Army and the King.

(He puts the point of his sword to the General's throat.)

Now, listen. Either I win these battles, or we all go down to hell together. That's how *that* works! For my part, General, I will stay in school. I will learn your strategy, you will learn to obey my orders! Now, get me back on that battlefield!

(They go into the smoke, leaving Frederick under the screens, which show us tangles of men and horses in combat. Explosions. Screams. Onto the stage staggers the Lieutenant, his face torn by shrapnel, and with one arm missing. He goes to his knees and cries out in mortal agony. Two soldiers run to his side and help to lift him upright and carry him off. As they go, they pass by the King, and once again Frederick and the Lieutenant face each other in the positions of the Prince and the young man he loved. The Lieutenant recognizes his hero, holds out his one arm to him, and screams.)

FREDERICK   Die quietly, can't you?

(Smoke. All disappear into it. The sounds of war die down. In a moment we hear a flute, playing the song of the Prince, composed years ago. As the smoke rises, soldiers drag on a destroyed cannon, and leave it turned on its side. A cart is brought on, and left. A brazier is set up, a fire lit, and soldiers bed down by it. Frederick enters, playing his flute, behind him Fredersdorf, carrying maps and papers. Without stopping his playing,

*Frederick nods, and Fredersdorf places papers, maps,
pen, and a bottle of ink on the upturned cart. The King
sits on the destroyed cannon, and plays, glancing down at
the papers. Moonlight, a shaft appearing upstage. Into
it walks Voltaire, holding two theatrical masks, one face
comic and benign, the other tragic and tormented. He
looks first at one, then the other, wryly. He puts first
one, then the other in front of his face. On the screen,
the hands passing a letter from one to another. Voltaire
holds down his masks, and looks at Frederick, who faces
out, playing his flute, glancing at his papers. When
Voltaire speaks, Frederick plays for a moment, smiling,
then breaks off to listen.)*

VOLTAIRE   The Prince who loves philosophy and music is
now the King who loves humanity. But that same Frederick bathes Europe in blood, reduces it to poverty, all
the time making verses and playing that flute. What are
we poor mortals to think of you, now that you outstrip
not only Marcus Aurelius, but also Genghis Khan?

*(Frederick puts down his flute, looks out, and answers
with the same sad, wry affection.)*

FREDERICK   Because, in the fashion of a good Christian, I
am about to destroy a city, or be destroyed myself, you
despair. But if I attacked the Vatican tomorrow instead
of Kesseldorf, and hung the Pope up by his heels, you
would rejoice, write an Ode to Freedom, and call me a
hero. Quite ridiculous. We philosophers and poets can
no more escape our preposterous human natures than
anyone else. You must allow my youthful ideals some
practical modification. Men condemn in the evening
what they approved in the morning; so much for European alliances. We go to war and spill our blood, yet the
glorious victory remains the same woman after we have
won her, only now she wears her nightcap, deposits her

false teeth in a jar, and rattles her trinkets when we try to sleep; so much for the national glory. From how many points of view may the same object be seen, philosopher?

VOLTAIRE   Philosopher, from which point of view will you choose to look?

FREDERICK   From the only one possible. The view produced by the corruption of the age. It is the only vision a decent man can have. And it is the morality of kings, which the decent must accept, to grant each other the right to seek only their own advantage. They are the first to chuckle at treaties, which are quite simply lies. Perhaps the age ahead that you seek so earnestly to enlighten will hold honesty in some esteem; this one does not. I am not defending my statecraft to you; I merely explain why every ruler is obliged to act deceitfully, and misuse his power.

VOLTAIRE   *(Gazing at his masks)*   But, my author of the *Anti-Machiavel*, must he do so with such obvious relish?

FREDERICK   Yes, otherwise he could not do it at all. Any man who rules a nation becomes, in time, a maniac. The only victory over that is to be aware of it.

VOLTAIRE   Are you, my Lord, aware of it?

FREDERICK   I think so. I was well schooled in lunacy, and in all the household origins of global treachery. My military strategy is, I admit, a bit radical, but I know what I am after. I am learning. I have made and broken alliances in tune with the rest of Europe, and the diplomats, those postmen, no longer talk back to me. I am very much at home, you see, in spite of my blunders, and my haste, which is extreme. I will win this war. I will win because I alone understand how desperate everything is. That

every moment is a matter of life and death. I have
learned my lessons, you see.

VOLTAIRE   I cannot match a poet who also leads an Army,
or a king whose music is as dazzling as his sword. Your
experience in life is unique. No man can speak with all
the astounding authority you alone possess.

FREDERICK   This war will not last forever. When it's over,
I will break my sword. I will go home, and be tame. I
won't so much as attack a cat.

VOLTAIRE   *Then* you will be Frederick the Great, and all
your battles truly won. Our strategy might be to dis-
solve not only the Holy Roman Empire, but also the
gunpowder of human anger. We might attempt to repress
not only one thousand petty European wars, but also
hold back the bursting waters of confused political pride.
Lead us to victory on these battlefields, and I will die
at the feet of the man who remains my hero.

FREDERICK   Watch and see. But not from so far away. When
are you coming to live with me? You will have to, sooner
or later. My court is the only place that can tolerate you.

*(Voltaire holds up the two masks and makes them bow
to each other.)*

VOLTAIRE   I look forward to the day when my obligations
here will permit it. I have the honor, at this moment, to
remain your Majesty's devoted servant, in France.

(He bows and disappears.)

FREDERICK   Devoted, if I win. A servant, hardly. But I will
possess you, great man. Wait and see.

(He looks about, smiles, takes up his flute, and begins to play again. Clouds pass over the moon, and the stage is dappled in a soft light. The Lieutenant enters, looking very puzzled.)

LIEUTENANT   *(Softly)*   Your Majesty.

FREDERICK   Yes, yes.

LIEUTENANT   Your Majesty, the Queen is here.

FREDERICK   I beg your pardon?

LIEUTENANT   The Queen is here. Yes, here, in camp. She has just arrived. She told me very firmly that she must see you. Now.

FREDERICK   You've lost your mind.

LIEUTENANT   It's true, Sire, really. She's adamant. What shall I tell her?

FREDERICK   Why, my old cow. Christ in heaven, Solomon had a thousand wives and they weren't enough. I have one, and that's one too many. All right, bring her here. Get her something to sit on, and some brandy and coffee for me.

(The Lieutenant goes. Frederick writes on his papers. Fredersdorf brings a chair, and then the Lieutenant escorts the Queen, who now stands before her husband. They leave her standing there. Frederick keeps writing, then looks up and shakes his head and smiles.)

FREDERICK   Well?

(In her heavy traveling clothes, the Queen stands trembling before him. She is a very awkward and very plain

woman. She has never in her life opposed anyone. She is very unsure of herself, but now is preposterously determined.)

THE QUEEN   I have been told that your losses have been terrible. That you are in great danger of losing the war. I thought you might let me see you, and I determined I would come and ask you for this audience. I am your wife. This is the only time I have asked it of you, after all.

(Frederick slaps his pen down on the papers and turns to her.)

FREDERICK   Now that's the truth. You have always been the most faithful creature in the universe, and I owe you the respect you demand. But I must confess I am astonished at you for getting up the gumption to demand it, and I have fought four battles in two months and I'm tired. You really must be quick.

THE QUEEN   I will try.

(Fredersdorf and the Lieutenant bring in a table with brandy, a coffeepot, and cups. Fredersdorf will serve, and then sit in the shadows. The Queen sits in the chair, and begins, with painful embarrassment. Frederick pours coffee, and listens.)

THE QUEEN   *(Stammering)* Is . . . is . . . my husband well?

FREDERICK   Oh, madam, please.

THE QUEEN   I beg your pardon. I can't . . . you . . . this isn't easy for me.

FREDERICK   I knew you'd begin that way, God bless you.
You are being very brave, just like a soldier. I know
what it means for you to come to see me. Compose yourself, and say what you came to say. Coffee?

THE QUEEN   No, thank you. But I will take some brandy,
if I may.

FREDERICK   *(Amazed)*   My dear woman, the next thing I
know you will grab my sword and rush off to fight my
enemies. What has come over you?

THE QUEEN   Oh, no, nothing has come over me. There have
been no miraculous transformations. I am still the igno-
rant and ugly girl your father picked for you, from a
sheepish crowd of dowdy virgins. But since our marriage, I have pleased myself to work as hard as I could,
with these clumsy hands and these slow wits, to be your
queen . . .

(She stops, falters.)

FREDERICK   That's well said. You've composed your speech
thoroughly. Drink a little brandy and continue. I'll wait.

THE QUEEN   I always knew I could never be a queen. Or
worthy of you. Your . . . neglect . . . and you must
admit it has been breath-taking in its . . . complete-
ness . . . like your other activities . . . well, I have
taken it as another shameful matter of course, in this
life of mine. I watch your greatness with agony and patience, and my pitiful lessons in embroidery and French
have never stopped, not in seven years. That is a long
time to study embroidery and French. Now I am getting
older and uglier, if that is possible. I have given up my
hope for children. Not heirs, simply children. I suppose
I might have had those by a coachman; perhaps you

wouldn't have minded at all. But no, I am still the same miserable girl, on my knees each night, praying to our Heavenly Father for the love and safety of my husband. Surely I have aroused your disgust by now.

(She smiles and drinks. His expression of polite attention does not change. She looks at him as a woman might at a brother she met only once, in childhood.)

But now, I find that I am beginning to laugh, as you do, when I think of certain things. My loutish ignorance, you see, is being simply worn away, not corrected by study or experience at all, but by sheer time and age, and all my frantic girlish fears go with it. Yesterday, when I heard you were almost killed, I could not keep from laughing. I remembered the first day we met, when I was dragged up before you by your father. Do you?

FREDERICK   Do I what, madam?

THE QUEEN   Remember that day?

FREDERICK   Well, I do now, thanks to this visit.

THE QUEEN   My father told me what to say, but he was as frightened as I was, poor man. And so I thought I would be myself, and trust to your understanding, and I stammered out to you my love of the church and my devotion to God. And in a minute, you said, not five feet away from me, clearly, to someone, "Jesus Christ, I would rather marry the biggest whore in Berlin than a pious woman."

(She drinks, and smiles.)

That has become, in the barbaric fullness of time, dear to me.

FREDERICK   Please. I cannot help the trick fate has played on me.

THE QUEEN   Ah, what trick is that? Is that why, timid and oafish spinster that I am, I find myself among soldiers and guns and war in the middle of the night, as in a melodrama for children? Perhaps I am not a woman at all, only a boy in disguise. Shall I now throw off these clothes and arouse something else besides seven years of the King's disgust? Would that be dramatic enough?

FREDERICK   Please, do not disgrace yourself.

THE QUEEN   No. I never have. I never will. But I can come to you, within all proper bounds, as I do tonight with the Austrian guns at your head, and ask for my place. I wish to leave my castle that you so graciously built for me at the other end of Prussia, and accept with you whatever defeat you face. That is queenly, you must admit.

FREDERICK   I do admit it. But it is not possible.

THE QUEEN   Why, in the name of heaven? Do you think I will mind, now, a husband who hates women? Do you think, while your kingdom crumbles around you, that I will scream at you because you have pretty page boys and handsome lieutenants in for breakfast? You have no qualms about the acrid scandal of your behavior—you even encourage it—do you think I will give you a sermon on the matter? I implore you, let me go back to the place where we should live, and be no longer the same ridiculous figure as a queen I always was as a girl! Give me at least the protection of those walls, if nothing else! Is that outrageous?

FREDERICK   *(Coldly)*   Yes. Is there anything else?

THE QUEEN   There is. And you will hear it now, from my own mouth. I am a wife remarkable for her loutish stupidity, as you have said yourself, while treating me with perfect civility. I will not be civil now, I will be direct. Your table talk may be scandalous, but your bedroom, so I am told, is monastic. I do not believe your masquerades with page boys and soldiers. They did not ring true to me seven years ago; they don't now. So I ask you, if you must banish me back into the convent you have made of my life, to satisfy at least my female curiosity. And to forgive your wife one outburst of temper in seven barren years.

FREDERICK   Are you all right?

THE QUEEN   *(With scorn)*   Öh, please. Please.

FREDERICK   Fredersdorf.

(Fredersdorf comes forward.)

FREDERICK   The Doctor, if you please. At once.

(Fredersdorf goes. The Queen lifts her head. She is miserably ugly now, crying, and she is a little drunk.)

FREDERICK   I have always respected you for the brave acceptance of a miserable fate, being married to me. I respect you no less now, for demanding a reason for that fate. You shall have it.

(The Doctor enters.)

FREDERICK   The Queen of Prussia, Doctor, wishes to know why it is that her husband, the King, has never consummated their union. Tell her.

DOCTOR   *(Under his breath)*   My God.

FREDERICK   Your embarrassment is altogether understandable. Take a minute to compose yourself. Then tell her the truth.

(He moves back to the upturned cart, by the destroyed cannon. He smiles and picks up the flute, in shadow, so that we cannot see his face. The Queen looks at the Doctor, and waits.)

FREDERICK   She is waiting.

(He begins to play, very softly, on the flute. The Doctor begins slowly, with painful hesitation, then speaks plainly, as if about any ordinary patient.)

DOCTOR   The King, as a young man, accompanied his father to the court of Poland. It was a licentious and immoral spectacle. His father's restraint was excessive. The young Prince, given at last the occasion, indulged himself in an excusable abundance of sexual pleasure. The King of Poland himself supplied the women. There were a great many of them.

(He pauses, clears his throat. From the shadows, Frederick breaks off his gentle music, and speaks quietly, then resumes.)

FREDERICK   Go ahead.

DOCTOR   *(Calmly)*   One was diseased. When the Prince returned to Prussia, he discovered that he was infected with a gonorrhea maligna. Caught in a boy's panic, ravaged by fears of his father discovering this hideous disgrace, the young Prince, in torment, submitted to the treatment of a doctor from Malchow, a quack. The treatment seemed successful. A few months passed. Then, doubled, the banked fires of the infection broke out again. In

further panic, and now in real danger of gangrene, the
Prince abandoned himself to more heroic treatment. He
was operated upon. Badly. The incision left him, as a
man, disabled. The infection was arrested, the disease
continued its course. Not long afterward, you were married to him.

*(The King's flute is silent. He moves out of the shadows,
looks at the Queen, and smiles.)*

FREDERICK   You see, everything has a reason. You are
quite right about my page boys. And my poems, and my
table talk. It is a masquerade. But Europe must believe
that the King of Prussia goes to bed with someone. Con-
clude, Doctor.

DOCTOR   Since his operation, his Majesty has not been able
to bring himself to attempt the sexual act.

FREDERICK   Thank you.

(The Doctor leaves.)

FREDERICK   Are you speechless now, all over again?

THE QUEEN   Yes.

FREDERICK   Well, I admire your persistence, after seven
years.

(The Queen rises.)

THE QUEEN   I will go home. I won't bother you again. And
I will pray to God that I never, never cause anyone to
lose any happiness as long as I live.

FREDERICK   *(Coldly, politely)*   That is both noble and gen-
erous. I regret I have already lost ours. Good night.

(The Queen stares at him, makes a helpless, numb gesture, and leaves. Frederick motions to the Doctor, who has been standing some distance away, to accompany her. He watches them go for a moment. There is a muffled explosion in the distance. He moves back into the shadows, and picks up his flute, plays softly. The Doctor now returns, moving through the dappled moonlight that leaves Frederick in shadow. The Doctor stands watching Frederick.)

FREDERICK   Yes?

DOCTOR   Is it true?

FREDERICK   Pardon?

DOCTOR   Is it the truth? I have never examined you, after all. As far as I know, no one has. You have told me what happened to you. If I outlive you, I will publish it. I suppose it is what you have decided to make known about yourself, in years to come. But is it the truth?

FREDERICK   Everyone is full of courage tonight. It must be an epidemic. My poor old cow races through battle-fields, and now you want to look at the balls of the King of Prussia.

(He smiles at the Doctor. Far away, there is another muffled explosion.)

God help you if you let that little publication go before I'm dead. If you outlive me, that's another matter. Write your book then, and put what you please in it. Good night.

(The Doctor bows and leaves. There is another far-off explosion, and a red glow tinges the moonlit sky. The soldiers are up, ragged and weary. They push the cart

and the cannon off. The cabinet enters, looking ominous.
They form their circle around the King.)

FREDERICK   Yes, yes, yes? Breathing fire, everyone?

CHANCELLOR   The Treasury is absolutely exhausted, Sire.
There is no more money.

FREDERICK   Melt the silver plate. Refine it for bullets.

BISHOP   The people pray for you no longer. You are the
devil now, the Anti-Christ.

GENERAL   The Army is very uneasy. Soldiers desert now
by battalions.

DOCTOR   Your health is shattered and you know it. You
don't eat and you don't sleep. You will collapse in a
month.

FREDERICK   *(Getting up)*   Yes, yes, yes, we are riddled
with holes, my little kingdom and I. Can't sleep, can't
eat. We are like pregnant women, filled with strange desires, but nothing helps. But what, gentlemen, am I going to do about it? Wash my face and hands and be
marched upstairs to bed like a good child? We fight today! Christ or Anti-Christ, I don't believe in either one.
I will be buried under the ruins of every building in
Austria before I yield to anyone! As for the soldiers who
desert, I will shoot them myself, by the battalion, if
I have to! March, damn you, gentlemen, right now,
march!!!

(Explosion and smoke, into which they vanish. The smoke
begins to clear. There is no sound. On the bare stage, they
all stand, apart from each other. A final, distant thump
of an explosion. The smoke is blown away, curling about

their legs. Silence. They all face one direction, Frederick in front with his sword in his hand. Silence. They look. Silence)

LIEUTENANT Why don't they attack?

GENERAL I don't know.

(They stare. Frederick moves. His body relaxes.)

FREDERICK I do. They're afraid.

(His face twists with a sardonic smile of achievement.)

They are afraid. Of me.

FREDERICK *(He is soft now, almost indolent.)* They won't attack. I knew what I was doing after all. Go to sleep. When I feel like it, I'll chase them home to their pretty young Queen. Send the dispatches. It's over.

(Organ, choir, a Te Deum. Frederick cocks his head, listens, is very pleased. He counts the beats, approves the music. The Bishop brings him a huge Bible. He takes it, laughing, and flips the pages, moving to the platform upstage. They face him. He searches, finds his passage, proclaims:)

"Let the woman learn in silence with all subjection. For I suffer a woman not to teach, nor to usurp authority over the man, but to be in silence." Timothy one, chapter two, verses eleven and twelve.

(He slaps the Bible shut and tosses it to the Bishop. He stretches and yawns.)

And now we have a bigger kingdom to manage. We will manage it. We will work harder in peace than ever we fought in war! But today, like frivolous mortals, let us enjoy the fruits of victory.

*(He strides down from the platform. But he is inter-
cepted at center stage by soldiers carrying a cot. On it
lies Fredersdorf. He breathes with great difficulty.)*

Fredersdorf! Fredersdorf! My God, what's wrong with
you?

*(In open distress he runs to the cot. Fredersdorf holds out
a shaking hand, and the King grabs it, with fervent and
unself-conscious emotion, and grips it tightly.)*

What? What? What's wrong?

FREDERSDORF   Why, I have given out, that's all. Did you
think I would be about forever, for you to take care of?

FREDERICK   Don't speak that way to me! Doctors, the doctors!

FREDERSDORF   I've seen them all. They smile and nod, yes,
it's true, when a man can't breathe, when he is as old
and sick and tired as I am, then he can't lift his head,
and he dies. That's all there is to it, it seems.

FREDERICK   I won't hear that! Bear up, for God's sake! It's
an order, old man!

FREDERSDORF   Now, now. Don't make my last act my only
disobedience. I don't want to leave you, after all.

FREDERICK   *(Weeping openly)*   Don't you? Don't you,
my friend?

FREDERSDORF   No. Listen, now, your Majesty, you must not
eat so many spices, do you hear me? You must stop load-
ing your plate with spices. It isn't good for you.

(He dies.)

FREDERICK   *(In anguish)*   I will try to remember.

(Soldiers carry Fredersdorf away. The King slumps and almost falls. A soldier reaches toward him to hold him. The King clenches his fists, grinds his teeth, smiles a ghastly smile.)

FREDERICK   Never mind. I am quite used to it. And Fortune may send me another friend.

(Harshly)

Let my victory celebrations proceed!

(He moves regally to one side of the stage in a grand and solemn procession. Around him gathers the cabinet. Frederick looks about, savoring the luxury of the spectacle. We become aware of night and candles and lamps. The night wind blows, softly. The dark sky becomes lit by lamps, by forty thousand of them, all moving, all revolving in slow circular rotation: it is a carrousel, like those of Louis XIV, but even more grandiose. We hear Frederick's music, arranged for full orchestra, in a suite to mark the occasion of the Austrian defeat and Prussian victory.

Voices rise, fall, buzz; a cluster of them break into clarity: we hear the repetition of a name, a name that gives feverish excitement to the voices, the most famous name in Europe: "Voltaire, Voltaire! Voltaire, Voltaire!"

He appears, opposite Frederick. A commoner, dressed quietly in plain clothes, he leans on a cane and gazes about, the absolute center of his world, the undisputed master of his age. He is the intellectual monarch of the Western world and the creator of European liberalism. And he has finally come to the court of his "disciple," the King of Prussia, to live with him as Royal Chamberlain.

Now, Voltaire stands before Frederick, and begins to kneel. Beaming with a flushed pride and a genuine pleasure, Frederick kneels with him. From a pocket, he takes a bright silver medal attached to a beautiful red ribbon. It is the seal of the King's Chamberlain, but also looks very much like the decoration given long ago to the boy by Fredersdorf. Frederick decorates his Voltaire, then lifts him up, clasps him in his arms with fierce joy. He grips his bony shoulders, pounds him on the back, fondles him, beaming. The two are caught in this moment of genuine delight, tasting their fame and the increase of it by this union. They beam, the people cheer, the music plays gaily, the bright lamps and a shower of royal fireworks dazzle the eyes; the explosions now are welcome and friendly, the reflected colors brilliant. Frederick continues to clasp the shoulders of his philosopher, and the philosopher continues to grin at his hero. A tremendous cheer from the crowd, a swift burst of music, and then a dazzling, blinding array of fireworks over them all.

Darkness. Wind, rain, a desolate stage, peopled suddenly by two crouched and solitary figures where only a second ago we saw the brilliance of the past. Sleet, thunder. A sighing of wind and a creaking of icy branches.

The two soldiers, with shovels, peer about on the darkened stage.)

SOLDIER 1   Are you sure you know which one it is?

SOLDIER 2   Yes, yes. Fourth over from the left. See, the dirt is fresh. Hurry!

SOLDIER 1   What if we dig up the wrong one?

SOLDIER 2   Then God help us.

SOLDIER 1   Ah, it's awful. The thing is an animal. A bloody, rotten animal. My God, what's it going to smell like, look like?

SOLDIER 2   We'll see soon enough. What was her name, I wonder. Did you know?

SOLDIER 1   No.

SOLDIER 2   Well, ready?

SOLDIER 1   Ready.

(There is the unmistakable sound of a real shovel crunching down into real earth. Behind the two gravediggers looms the great horse, and its shadow falls upon them. Above, as all the lights die, we see the frantic shadow of the old man, vanishing as he goes by us, galloping across the screen.)

Act 3
The Philosopher

(During the intermission, Frederick's Symphonia in D for Orchestra has been heard. On the screen, throughout, the portrait by Menzel of "The Flute Concert."
The lights fade. On the screen, the shadow of the old man riding moves with the beat of the snare drums. The wooden horse moves onto the edge of the stage and stops. The figure on its back, in shadow, sits motionless as before, watching.
Lights up on a dining room in Sans Souci, Frederick's palace in Potsdam. We see a table, placed in the exact spot where we saw Frederick William's "Tobacco Parliament" table, but this one is not a rough wooden arrangement: it is a circular, gilded table of glittering beauty, and the chairs placed around it are exquisite. To one side, a long table with decanters of delicate crystal holding wines.
Offstage, we hear the tinkle of a clavichord and the song of a flute. Onto the stage walks Voltaire, bored, moving slowly and listlessly. His carbuncle eyes are dull, his waggish, toothless mouth firmly shut. With him, talking, is a guest, an Italian historian, played by the same actor who played the painter in Act One. He is florid, loquacious, and dull.)

HISTORIAN . . . and so I joined a joyful family of two parents, four older brothers, three older sisters, and a Great Dane. Time then passed, and I had a sister.

(Voltaire yawns.)

VOLTAIRE   Who had the Great Dane?

HISTORIAN   I beg your pardon?

VOLTAIRE   Forgive me, sir. I was not listening. I lose all ability to concentrate within range of that flute. Too much flute music, you understand, deranges.

HISTORIAN   Does he play this long every day?

VOLTAIRE   Each and every one, unless he is galloping off for an evening's drill. I have heard more concerti, sonatas, mournful adagios, and elegant cadenzas in the past two years than in all the days of my life, and all of it, all, exactly the same.

HISTORIAN   But very charming, you will admit.

VOLTAIRE   Oh, yes. Quickly.

HISTORIAN   Perhaps his Majesty's music is like many beautiful women, delightful but occasionally long-winded.

VOLTAIRE   Very perceptive. In any case, one might do better with less music and more women.

(Smiling quickly)

As I heard someone else say, somewhere, some long time ago, who is no longer with us, and in fact probably didn't say anything of the kind, at all.

(The Historian nods absently, looks around with awe and admiration. Voltaire takes a glass. A steward pours wine.)

HISTORIAN   Sans Souci! The Emperor's retreat!

VOLTAIRE   Yes, here we live, in isolated elegance. You approve?

HISTORIAN   It is a thrilling tour de force of taste, elegance, and beauty.

VOLTAIRE   Yes, it is all quite rapturous. Supper parties are delicious. The furniture is perfect.

(Pause)

HISTORIAN   I am not sure I understand you.

VOLTAIRE   I take care to see you don't.

(Listens)

What a deafening silence. He must have stopped playing. Yes, yes, the evening begins.

(Enter Frederick, laughing, with his cabinet and Moreau de Maupertuis, a large and pompous man, who wears a huge red wig. Frederick is in very good spirits.)

FREDERICK   Surprise, Voltaire! Surprise, surprise.

VOLTAIRE   I am alarmed, Sire. What surprise would your Majesty call surprising?

FREDERICK   I have just discovered a long-lost oil portrait of you. In a lot of junk brought over from the old palace in Berlin. It's a perfect likeness, absolutely. Some unknown prophet must have painted it years ago. It's being brought to you now. You'll see.

(To the Historian)

My dear friend, delighted to see you. Your Persian History is superb. I've just had it bound for my library.

HISTORIAN   Too kind, too kind.

FREDERICK   Now we'll sit down to dinner, chat a bit, and
hope to make you feel at home. Have you met these gentlemen?

*(Frederick guides the Historian toward the cabinet, and
turns privately to Voltaire.)*

FREDERICK   I have missed you. You stay away from my table
too long.

VOLTAIRE   My work, Sire. Your sole rival for my affection.

FREDERICK   And the only one whose victories I suffer with
patience. But not with pleasure. But never mind.

(He turns to Maupertuis.)

And now our academic contingent is complete. Gentlemen, Monsieur de Maupertuis has consented to become
the President of my Academy of Science. He honors us all.
We must also congratulate him on the publication of his
latest work. Brilliant, brilliant.

(Everyone except Voltaire applauds.)

MAUPERTUIS   I thank your Majesty most humbly.

FREDERICK   I am referring, gentlemen, to the pamphlet "On
Happiness," by our distinguished colleague. Everyone is
tremendously impressed by it. Except Voltaire, of course.
He says it's very dry and miserable and doesn't make
anyone happy who has to read it.

MAUPERTUIS   I have composed my work for the glory of
Almighty God and the King of Prussia. I will leave it
to them to judge its merit.

FREDERICK   Exactly what I told Voltaire. I said we will allow the Almighty final judgment on the book. He said, well, yes, perhaps God Almighty will be able to understand it.

(Laughter. Frederick shakes his head in mock bewilderment.)

I tell you, gentlemen, dealing with poets and philosophers is a ticklish business. More trouble than fifty kingdoms. If I wanted the world to be truly miserable, I think I might have it governed by writers. What do you think, Voltaire?

VOLTAIRE   Since his Majesty is himself a poet, I cannot help but agree with him.

FREDERICK   *(To the Historian)*   I hope you notice, dear friend, that here everyone says exactly what he thinks. Just like a tavern. To table, gentlemen. No servants to bother us. We'll have some wine, chat, and then dinner will be brought along.

(They are at their places. Frederick lifts his glass for a toast. He is now forty, but, as always, looks older. He is unkempt, and dirty. His uniform is old, in one place patched. It is stained with snuff. He can still be gracious and truly charming, but his movements are more abrupt, his angers, when they come, more arbitrary, and his sarcasm much deeper.)

FREDERICK   To the Holy Roman Empire, gentlemen, an ancient institution, a bit senile, even, and to the part Prussia must surely play in its future. To Change, which is inevitable, and to Chance, the chief instrument in that change. And oh, yes, indeed, gallantry insists, to the three great empresses of Europe: Maria Theresa, Elizabeth, Pompadour—their babies, their lovers, their venereal diseases—and their shocking female lust for the body of our nation! The Empire!

(A chorus of your Majesties, and they all drink and sit down. Voltaire, in mock puzzlement, pretends confusion, sits slower than the others, and gains the attention.)

VOLTAIRE   That is a very covered dish, your Majesty. And the odd mixture inside is fascinating. Do you think we might have another look before we dine?

HISTORIAN   And the Empire, if I may say so, is neither Holy nor Roman.

VOLTAIRE   Indeed, as I believe Diderot remarked, some twenty years ago. No, it is the collected works of this editor Chance that his Majesty salutes. But I wonder, Sire, if you are thinking of still another edition of this great cookbook?

FREDERICK   Well, a few bindings are loose. Yes, I have my editor's instincts. I do wonder if a few chapters might not be rearranged slightly. The future will inform us, but for the present, our dish remains covered. At dinner, the guest must trust his host. Your health.

VOLTAIRE   But zounds! as they say in England. A clumsy servant upsets the dish. Gunpowder soup? Boot-leather pie? Bullet shells in the salad, war directives among the lettuce leaves? And what, then, is the tender, succulent beefsteak? I shudder to think! This red wine? Horrors! Do not tell us, Sire, that the poet, the musician, the tireless administrator will now put on his military apron again and serve us our fellow men for supper!

FREDERICK   I am the luckiest of poets. I have my verses criticized by Voltaire himself. "Pooh, this is worthless.

Wipe this out for the love of God. This can pass, this is tolerable, this is good." Once I remember: "Here you must be bold, Sire. Heroic! Strike!"

(He chuckles.)

But now, when I think in terms of Europe in precisely the manner he wishes me to think about verses, he quavers, shudders, turns blue. With envy, perhaps, as well as alarm. Come, come, admit it. If you attacked the world with the same ferocity that you attack your immortal verses—and, by the way, anyone who suggests they are less than immortal—why, you would shed more blood in a day than I in a lifetime of war!

(Much approval from the cabinet. Voltaire smiles brightly.)

VOLTAIRE   Verses, Sire, even bad ones, are always heroic, for their cause is enlightenment. Battles never are, for their cause is human destruction. They may be awesome, like cannibals, but never heroic.

FREDERICK   *(To Historian)*   You see? The King of Prussia is told off in good round terms. Freedom, no?

(To Voltaire)

Oh, my fierce friend. I have often tried to imagine you with a sword instead of a pen, but it's hopeless. There is nothing more comical, gentlemen, than Voltaire before an illness or the idea of death. The fearless advocate of human rights is then the immediate plaything of panic terrors. He conjures up a thousand red-eyed devils, all waiting to seize him. You will certainly hear that at point of death he called in all the parish priests and father confessors within fifty miles. He will dishonor us all.

VOLTAIRE   Who can say, my Lord, what a man will do on that interesting day?

BISHOP   I am thunderstruck! Has his Majesty succeeded in proving Voltaire pious after all? Perhaps not in the spirit or the intellect, but in the ordinary and perishable flesh?

FREDERICK   Have I?

VOLTAIRE   Not for a moment.

(To the Bishop)

I am sorry to disappoint you, but no, I am not really pious. At least not so pious as the Egyptians, who worshiped crocodiles and onions. Nor so pious as those Holy Fathers who employ infantile stagecraft to dominate the mind and scrub the pocketbook of the poor and innocent. I cannot accept the divinity of the brave young Jew who supposed himself Dionysus reborn, and I suspect all those who tell me I should be pious, for I am quite at ease in my opinion that they know no more about the matter than I or anyone else. Like poor, puzzled Job, I am always flabbergasted at men who have the effrontery, not to mention the bad taste, to speak for God.

MAUPERTUIS   That's because you want to do that yourself. A form of jealousy, you know, not uncommon in great men.

BISHOP   You see, gentlemen, Voltaire amuses us, and while we are laughing, he runs outside to nail up the doors of the church.

VOLTAIRE   Not at all. Let us have public worship. Let us meet—well, three or four times a year—in some grand temple, with music, and thank God for all his gifts. There is one sun, there is one God; let us have one religion. Then, perhaps, we may approach brotherhood, forgive each other our private monstrosities; and heavens

—is it possible?—fulfill the strange and beautiful dreams of our Dionysian Jew.

FREDERICK   Horse shit. I will desert and join the Bishop. It is indecent, when you have a reputation for wit, to spoil a supper by telling us that all men are brothers. Is this what comes, finally, from Voltaire's kitchen? If it is my fate to serve up a roast of my enemies' flesh, is that any more absurd than your bland soup, fizzing with unphilosophical bromides like brotherly love? You make us all ill. Men eat flesh. It serves the body. I didn't sign that into law; it's the way things are. Flesh is eaten, but eat brotherly love, dear friends, as some of us must pretend to do now and then, and help! nausea soon follows.

VOLTAIRE   But if we devour each other, Sire, who will be left to drink wine, make jokes, and spin out whimsical images? I have never understood why monarchs are so bored with brotherly love and so infatuated by brotherly hatred.

FREDERICK   You know very well that we vomit brotherly love onto the council tables, and then go to the battle-fields to be cleansed of the mess. Gentlemen, gentlemen, pass a divining rod, please, over the sparkling words of the famous poet, and what do you always find lurking about there underneath—the palpitating engine that drives all that brilliance? Love. That, really, is what you preach, as wanton in philosophy as a whore in a dirty bed. Love each other. The madman in every artist babbles about it way down there in the mines below the surface. It is the last word of the fop, before he swallows the pistol barrel and blows off the top of his head. It is the final reproach of the lunatic, opening his veins. Love is the high priest of the suicide, and the final commandment of the insane!

VOLTAIRE Sire . . .

FREDERICK No, no! The body is honest if the mind is not. It vomits!

VOLTAIRE I will confess that I cannot, with reason, set upon mankind the commandments of love. I am hardly that optimistic, and no longer that erotic. Men cannot love each other. It is not in their nature to do so. How obvious. I cannot say, "Love each other," without being absurd, but I will say, I must say, and I do say, what they *can* do: "Stop killing each other!"

(Pause. Frederick smiles and shakes his head slowly.)

FREDERICK It is the same thing, my dear friend. One is just as impossible as the other. How many plans and schemes for eternal peace do you think float across my desk in a year? Like the leaves in autumn, believe me. And yours, my dear Voltaire, among the rest. Very practical proposals. They would work perfectly well. All that is needed, you understand, is the consent of Europe, and a few little things like that. No, man will never give up his right to violence. You might as well ask him— out of brotherly love—to castrate himself, for his violence is as necessary to him as his lust. Negotiation without weapons would be like music without instruments.

VOLTAIRE Then you leave us no hope at all.

FREDERICK Crossed swords, not brotherly love, may bring us into a miraculous age, but that alone will do it. Oh, any child anywhere knows this is the truth, why abuse our maturity by hypocritically beating this dead horse, peace among men, and a brother's love for his fellow insects. And really, there are some limits, after all, even to insults in a tavern. Our guest, our guest! We have neglected you shamelessly, dear friend. Tell us, how do you find life in Prussia?

HISTORIAN   Your Majesty's kingdom is the marvel of the Western world. It is a novel sensation to witness this marriage of Athens and Sparta.

FREDERICK   Pray don't forget to drag in Rome, Babylon, Egypt, and China.

HISTORIAN   I beg your Majesty's pardon?

GENERAL   His Majesty asks for frank opinions, not flattery. You are not at supper in the court of Austria. Speak up. What have you observed of our military, for instance?

VOLTAIRE   Be very specific, my dear sir.

HISTORIAN   I have noticed the splendid bearing of the soldiers and the great mystique of service instilled into the officers. It is a remarkable substitution for the privileges of the nobility. I wonder how it feels to be a military saint?

VOLTAIRE   *(Rolling his eyes)*   Not that specific.

(Brightly)

There is a new pastry much in vogue these days in Patagonia. Would your Majesty like to hear about it?

FREDERICK   No. Continue, eminent Historian, about the military.

HISTORIAN   *(Oblivious)*   Well, the soldiers, as I say, march and bear themselves wonderfully well. In full field equipment, they carry almost as much on their backs as the Roman soldier.

FREDERICK   Almost as much?

HISTORIAN   Yes, Sire. The Roman soldier, of course, had to carry his entire world on his back, and so he was superior in bearing up under sheer weight.

(Frederick motions quietly to the steward, whispers to him. He dashes off.)

HISTORIAN   However, the bearing and the carriage are much the same.

GENERAL   You went to war with Caesar, then, a few months ago?

HISTORIAN   *(Laughing)*   No, no, but I have made a close study of the Roman military. And I would have liked to go to war with Julius Caesar, that lion of commanders. There has surely never been anyone like him.

(Voltaire covers his face with one hand.)

FREDERICK   I think Julius Caesar was overrated. He had the advantage of that melodious name, for one thing, and the reputation for gallantry, for another. The legend is that when he won a battle, he feasted on his officers' wives, and nothing helps your reputation more than that. It is more likely, however, that Caesar was not the husband of all the married ladies of Rome, but, rather, the wife of all the husbands.

(Laughter. Two soldiers come in quickly, carrying a full set of a Prussian soldier's field equipment.)

FREDERICK   And now, my dear friend, since you are so eager to follow the wars, and are so certain of Roman superiority over Prussian, may I suggest that you try on our field equipment and see for yourself?

HISTORIAN   Is your Majesty serious?

VOLTAIRE   Of course not. Laugh, dear friend.

(The Historian sees that Frederick means it. He smiles, goes to the soldiers. Frederick is also smiling, but his voice is not pleasant.)

FREDERICK   Slap it to him.

(The soldiers attack the Historian roughly with packs, straps, and weapons.)

FREDERICK   How does it feel, my friend?

HISTORIAN   *(Staggering)*   Good, your Majesty. Very good.

FREDERICK   Yes, I thought you'd change your tune when you felt something substantial stuck up your ass. Criticism is easy, art difficult. Heavy enough?

HISTORIAN   I confess that it is, your Majesty.

FREDERICK   *(Glaring at Voltaire)*   But not so heavy as the burden of the man who puts it there. I am accused, at my own table, gentlemen, of being a bloodthirsty war lord!

(Nervous laughter, which Frederick silences)

Since it is the foremost writer of the age who says so, it is no laughing matter! Monsieur Voltaire, splendid critic of my awkward verses, accept from me, I beg you, one elementary lesson in continental politics. I keep my army strong, so does everyone else. I hoard money for my Treasury, so does everyone else. But simply because I piss on alliances more openly than most, and break tonight the promises of this morning, you stand up and call me a peculiar philosopher, a bloody tyrant! Why, to hell with you.

I keep my promises only as far as my strength allows. Who, tell me, is any different? Alliances? *Peace treaties?* They are marriage contracts! I promise to make war, or not to make war, just as the brave new husband promises to fuck his wife forever, and satisfy all her lusts. But, as in marriage, where that burning little cunt can so often soak up the husband's strength, so in continental negotiations of war, the bottomless demands of allies can make faithfulness intolerable. And when the husband is exhausted, nothing can keep the man from getting a divorce. Why labor the analogy? You are all accomplished politicians; you know what I mean.

(To Voltaire)

Have I reassured you, my dear friend?

VOLTAIRE   You replace all my doubts . . . with others.

FREDERICK   *(In cold anger)*   You must understand there are some impertinences denied even you, monsieur. You would be the first to forget your silly daydreams if you staggered under the weight of a kingdom, as I do.

(To the Historian, now strapped into all the equipment.)

Well, dear friend and famous historian, confess that a Prussian soldier carries heavier field equipment than a Roman soldier. True or false?

HISTORIAN   *(Wobbly)*   True, true. I was quite wrong.

FREDERICK   But you are still not complete. Here!

(Frederick jumps up from the table, grabs a rifle with fixed bayonet from one soldier, throws it into the Historian's hands, then snatches it back again. He repeats this, executes a skillful manual of arms, throws it to the Historian again, with great force. Now, in a manic

rhythm, he snatches and throws the rifle until the company must interrupt.)

VOLTAIRE   Your Majesty! Your Majesty! He is pale. Sire, I beg you.

GENERAL   I think that is right, Sire. The gentleman is quite pale.

FREDERICK   *(Wheeling about)*   And so am I, under the burdens I carry! Do you think I don't know what it feels like to stagger under that weight? Do you think I take on my duties as though they were the most natural things in the world, with a smile and a happy fart? When will . . .

(His eye now lights on the table holding the decanters of wine. He grabs at them, runs his hands over them, inspects them minutely. Then he explodes with fury.)

Four wines? Four wines? What are four wines doing here? It's diabolical. Who's responsible? Two wines, only two, before supper. I drew up the order myself! Where is that cock-sucking steward? Ridiculous! Waste! Waste!

(He storms out. We hear his voice raised in terrible anger, and the echoing, fearful replies of servants. The Historian, standing at strict attention, with all the field equipment bolted on over his elegant clothes, holds his rifle at attention, and weaves slightly. Everyone else is silent, staring straight ahead, in discomfort. Voltaire smiles, looks about, and observes the spectacle.)

VOLTAIRE   Are you still alive?

HISTORIAN   Yes.

VOLTAIRE   Then I shall make up a little dictionary for you, as used by those in power. "My friend" means "my slave." "My dear friend" means "I hate you," and "Have dinner with me tonight" means "I am going to take the skin off you to pass the evening."

HISTORIAN   Thank you.

VOLTAIRE   Not at all.

DOCTOR   Another fit of obscene frugality. Or frugal obscenity, as you please. Do you think we will ever get anything to eat?

GENERAL   Who can say? He ripped his coat yesterday, you know, took a pair of scissors, cut two inches off the bottom, and wears it tonight.

VOLTAIRE   Something else for you. He has just spent a great deal of money having my apartments redecorated. Walls and ceiling are one great, exquisite mural, but the subject is a tribe of monkeys. The Age of Reason, you understand.

CHANCELLOR   You must remember, monsieur, how much of all this was beaten into him as a child.

VOLTAIRE   *(Ironically)*   Oh, indeed, yes. Never have a father and a son been more unlike. Well, gentlemen, here we sit.

(To the Historian)

And there you stand. In this philosopher's paradise, where all is freedom and unshackled good sense. Isn't it delightful?

(Frederick enters, mopping his face with a kerchief, somewhat out of breath. He is smiling again.)

FREDERICK   Well, well, forgive my outburst. But those scoundrels in my kitchens will beggar me yet. But now, a pleasure, a pleasure. Gentlemen, the long-lost mystic portrait of Arouet de Voltaire has arrived. Painted God knows when by a seer, a visionary who foresaw the glory of the future.

(To Voltaire)

Are you ready for this revelation? The likeness may overwhelm you.

VOLTAIRE   I am quite ready, your Majesty, for anything.

FREDERICK   Splendid. Portrait of the great Voltaire! *Voilà!*

(Upon the screen we see again the painting of the monkey in the uniform done for Frederick William twenty-three years before. The grotesque caricature of the dressed-up animal stares out at us again, wearing glasses, holding a book, gesturing as if giving a lecture. Frederick, who does not remember where the portrait originated, laughs gaily, as do the others, with the exception of Voltaire, who is amazed at the coarse childishness of the joke.)

FREDERICK   Perfection! What accuracy, what detail! What a likeness! It's you, dear friend, and you must treasure this portrait and hang it in your apartment tonight!

MAUPERTUIS   Along with the rest of the monkeys in the mural! Brilliant! You see, Monsieur Voltaire, there is a purpose in everything done by the King of Prussia.

(Everyone enjoys Voltaire's discomfort.)

FREDERICK   Glorious. Well, gentlemen, continue your conversation. I really must attend to our guest. My dear

sir, have you been standing here long? Well, you'll forgive our little joke, surely. All in fun. Allow me, please.

*(With great charm, he helps the Historian out of the
field equipment, unbuckling and unstrapping the gear
with a practiced hand.)*

Go on, gentlemen, talk, talk. Or I will. You know, that
fine portrait of our great friend is so accurate it makes
an ordinary man wonder. Why do so many women
prostrate themselves before that figure? Who can answer that?

MAUPERTUIS   Who would want to? Voltaire's women. I cannot think of a more boring subject for free conversation,
especially if you include his niece, who really is a scat-
terbrain. Or even the famous and learned Madame du
Châtelet, may she rest in peace. *There* was an interesting
case.

FREDERICK   You knew her, didn't you?

MAUPERTUIS   Some years ago, your Majesty, yes.

FREDERICK   I thought so. What did you think of her? A
trifle bizarre, perhaps?

MAUPERTUIS   Just so, God bless her Newtonian soul. I always found her quite ridiculous as a woman.

VOLTAIRE   *(Quietly)*   I will defend her memory, your
Majesty. She was a woman of gallantry and intellect.

FREDERICK   Perhaps that is what made her ridiculous.

(To Maupertuis)

Wouldn't you say so?

MAUPERTUIS   Certainly. And that, your Majesty, is the answer to my riddle! It is just such strange ladies, whose senses are stimulated by the fingers of the intellect, who become Voltaire's prey and his comfort. What love-making! Talk, talk, scratch, scratch!

(Voltaire explodes.)

VOLTAIRE   What, Sire? What, Sire? The memory of the woman I loved for twenty years, a lady who died in my arms, is thus attacked in my presence? Spattered with the vile abuse of this red-wigged abortion of Parnassus, for whom she always showed the greatest kindness?

FREDERICK   Response?

MAUPERTUIS   Your silly mistress was kind to me once, true, and in order to pay her for her kindness, I had to go to bed with her. I can assure you that ordeal discharged all my obligations.

VOLTAIRE   *(Furious)*   You want war! We will have it!

(Frederick, finished with the Historian, a bayonet in his hands, moves to the table, throws the bayonet down in front of Voltaire and mocks him with savage delight.)

FREDERICK   Will you, indeed? And you are the great philosopher who informs me that I am a bloodthirsty war lord! You are the sweet, fragrant soul who knows how kingdoms should be ruled, and who preaches brotherly love to mankind, while you roast your own enemies alive! You make verse like a god, and have the character of a monkey! You disgust me down to the heels of my boots! And *that* is the philosophical truth, anyway! Isn't it? Well, gentlemen, converse! Talk, talk!!

(Frederick digs into his coat pocket, pulls out his snuff-box, jams snuff into his nose. He sneezes sloppily and convulsively, shakes his head, and wipes the front of his shirt with one hand. Then he sees Voltaire, still standing, gazing at him.)

Well, what are *you* looking at?

VOLTAIRE *(Slowly)* I shall look where I please.

(Frederick blinks his eyes, stunned.)

FREDERICK What did you say?

VOLTAIRE I must inform your Majesty that I shall look where I please.

(Frederick stares at him, as the gates of his memory swing open. Suddenly, he turns in his tracks and stares up at the portrait of the monkey on the screen, and remembers where it came from and what happened on that evening. He sags, looks about in confusion. His voice is a hushed whisper.)

FREDERICK I must regretfully bring this enjoyable conversation to an end. It has been a great pleasure. Dinner will be served to you somewhere else. Good evening.

(He stands mute, stricken by memory and fatality. Everyone gets up slowly and leaves, in great embarrassment. When he is alone, Frederick picks up the bayonet, cries out, lifts it high above his head, and brings it slashing down onto the gilded table. The lights go out, but once more the monkey in the uniform gapes out at us, then fades, as we hear the hoofbeats of the galloping horse and see the shadow pass across the screen.
Voltaire walks downstage and moves into a light. A

soldier carries a traveling cloak and swings it up onto his frail shoulders.)

VOLTAIRE Thank you. Please announce me to his Majesty.

(The soldier bows and moves into darkness. Voltaire paces up and down, listening to the sounds that come out of the darkness now: the far-off shouts and slaps and marching of troops drilling. Menzel battle etchings on the screen. Frederick appears upstage, his back to Voltaire, also pacing, watching his troops drill. Voltaire moves closer to him, waits. Frederick does not turn around.)

FREDERICK Yes?

VOLTAIRE I have come to pay my respects to your Majesty.

FREDERICK You insist, then, on this leave-taking?

VOLTAIRE My health and my work make it necessary, Sire.

FREDERICK Then I wish you a pleasant journey, monsieur.

VOLTAIRE Sire.

(He bows and starts to leave. Soldiers appear on the forestage. Voltaire looks at them quizzically. He turns back, and waits.)

FREDERICK We have a few things that belong to each other. They should be returned.

VOLTAIRE As you wish. To what does your Majesty refer?

FREDERICK My Chamberlain's seal. Begin with that.

VOLTAIRE   Here it is, on this ribbon around my throat. I had hoped to keep it, but, as you say, it is yours. What else?

FREDERICK   My trust. You cannot break a ribbon and return that so easily.

VOLTAIRE   Did I ever have it? You cannot trust your generals with your soldiers, your stewards with your wines, your judges with your laws, or your tax collectors with the people's money. If you threw a bone to a dog, you would track him down to be certain he chewed it in the prescribed manner and did not somehow deceive you.

FREDERICK   And you? You have not deceived me?

VOLTAIRE   I gave you my heart, Sire.

FREDERICK   *(Livid)*   Ah, yes, the worst part of yourself. You should have kept that and given me the rest! You insult my friends from under my wing. You talk to ambassadors of state affairs and parade your paltry, inept political dreams about. You publish a lethal satire against Maupertuis, the President of my Academy of Science, that literally buries him alive. And this after I read that wicked thing, laughed with you, and forbade its publication.

VOLTAIRE   You know it was stolen from me and published without my consent.

FREDERICK   That old song is a tin nightingale now. It bores me to death. You must yield to the fury of your shrill passions. Very well, I must also take steps. You leave me no choice. Be so good as to turn around.

(Out of the darkness steps the executioner, a torch in one hand.)

FREDERICK   What do you see?

VOLTAIRE   I see a common hangman, my Lord. What do you think you are doing?

FREDERICK   *(To the hangman)*   Execute your commission.

(The hangman exits.)

VOLTAIRE   It is always my great weakness to believe in the possibility of a philosophical king who manages to remain a human being. This is a grave flaw, one that is truly corrected only by hangmen, it seems.

(From offstage, a glow of flickering red light)

FREDERICK   So.

VOLTAIRE   Burn me? Burn me, Sire?

FREDERICK   Treacherous children must be punished. That is your infamous book being consumed. The entire edition is being burned to ashes.

(Now, when Voltaire turns from the blaze to face the King, he does so with a fierce, firelit smile.)

VOLTAIRE   This is the greatest honor you have yet bestowed on me. I am very much obliged to you, and so are all my books.

FREDERICK   I am appalled to see that a poet of your genius has the imagination of a sick child, who always expects too much. Of me, you created a phantom, who did not exist. Now you fill yourself with disgust because the King of Prussia does not please to live out your poetic dreams.

VOLTAIRE *(Hotly)* It is not in a dream that I now see
. a man who pretended to be a friend, but held his crown
in his pocket like a hoodlum with a pistol! No dream has
shown me your genius poisoned by a brutality that pours
gall into your soul, or this wretched pleasure you must
take in humiliating other men, a pleasure all the more
disgraceful since you are elevated so far above them all,
both by rank and that very imagination you now so
quaintly despise. Where has it come from, this black
wind that decays your bright spirit, and turns everything
into malice?

FREDERICK From God, in whom we are pleased not to believe. I know very well that I have faults, great faults.
You know I do not treat myself gently.

VOLTAIRE Ah, your Majesty, let that alone for now, I beg
you! This grand vocation as a hero and this posture as
a king have ravaged your heart, and this really is too
bad, my Lord, for without your heroism and your throne,
you could have been the most charming man in all the
world.

*(Frederick seizes the ribbon, breaks it, and tears the
seal from Voltaire's neck.)*

FREDERICK
Your lessons are poison, they will not heal;
I squeeze the lemon and throw away the peel.

VOLTAIRE *(Quietly)* I regret I cannot approve all your
verses, or change this course of your contempt for mankind.

(He moves away a few steps, stops, turns back.)

You know what will happen, of course. The world, that
hates to think, will say of us: "Philosophers are pompous

enough to tell us what to believe, but look at them, they cannot live in peace any more than we can. A king did not believe in Jesus Christ, and he called to his court a philosopher who didn't either, and they tore each other to pieces. There was no humanity in these pretended philosophers, and God punished one by means of the other." And the world we might have enlightened will sigh and nod and understand nothing. Good-by, philosopher.

FREDERICK   Philosopher, good-by.

(Voltaire bows and retires. Frederick draws himself straight, stares coldly ahead, listening to the drilling of his troops. In a moment, he looks down at the ribbon and the seal. In his hand, it looks like the ribbon and the medal given the child by Fredersdorf. He shivers.)

FREDERICK   Guard!

(A soldier appears.)

FREDERICK   Let my greyhounds out of the palace. I will walk with them in my gardens.

(Exit, swiftly. Sounds of marching feet grow louder. The cabinet moves to the front of the stage, with proclamations.)

GENERAL   His Majesty's spring maneuvers will continue indefinitely. All regiments will maintain activity at full strength. Let the world hear the sounds of Prussian drill, and take care.

(Drums, and, from far away, hoofbeats.)

CHANCELLOR   Well aware of the feminine intrigues of the empresses of Europe, and of their coalition to invade his kingdom, take from him his province of Silesia, and destroy him, his Majesty commands the only action open to a man of honor. He declares a state of war between this nation and Saxony, and Sweden, and Austria, and Russia, and France. The King crossed the borders of Saxony last night. He will be in Dresden in a week.

(Cannon fire, far off. On the screens above the cabinet, a dull red glow.)

DOCTOR   Prussians! The Empire, the continent, shake before you! Your spirit matches the valor of your great King, who strikes in every direction about him, his ferocity changing the face of war itself. Rossbach, Leuthen, Torgau! With two hundred thousand soldiers, he defeats forces holding together one hundred million men. By day our Monarch is the whirlwind, by night his music and his verses resound over the dark and bloody fields of death. Stir yourselves further! March with us to perdition for such a man!

(Gunfire, cannon fire, point-blank upon us. Flames of war blaze on the screens. A sound, low and steady, of the cries of people in flight and turmoil. The shadow of the horseman gallops across the screen. We hear the voice of Frederick, reciting his poetry.)

VOICE OF FREDERICK
War, be thou my sovereign good, let Fire convince
The soul of a King of the death of a Prince.

GENERAL   Commanders! Military Instructions of the King of Prussia, Section Five, Article 28, Item 4: When it is difficult to gain intelligence of the enemy, employ this cruel but necessary expedient. Seize a rich German burgher, possessed of lands, a wife, and children. Force him to go to the enemy, posing as a traitor. If he cannot return with the desired intelligence, burn his lands and his houses, and kill his family. It serves the purpose.

VOICE OF FREDERICK

> I fast embrace this tyrant of my mind,
> And soar to war on his great wing;
> Beneath us bloody wretches find,
> I think, I live, I die, a King.

BISHOP   From these days of wrath, we pray for deliverance and for the mercy of God. Around us we feel the dire hatred of Europe. Our King must face the great armies massed at our borders, ready now to circle closer and closer to hunt him down.

VOICE OF FREDERICK

> Man is born to act, and Thought declares him free,
> But Reason and his Passion disagree.
> A Universe removed, a King all life despises,
> His hand unswayed by a world's disguises.

DOCTOR   Kolin, Hochkirch, Kunersdorf. These disastrous defeats have cost us half our nation. Our homeland writhes in a holocaust of foreign invaders. Let us meet our fate with the terrible courage of our embattled Monarch.

VOICE OF FREDERICK

> A Prince has his dreams, a King his success,
> While the head from the body is torn;
> If you fancy this damned human race, confess,
> The King did not ask to be born.

LIEUTENANT   Prussians, his courage is inhuman; who can explain it? Incredible twists and turns to avert destruction, everlasting marches, impossible attacks, no comforts or luxuries for him, no, born to honor, he calls for torture, privation, blasted hopes, dead soldiers, and bloody hands. It is given to us to witness true greatness: stern, implacable, sublime. Glory forever to the King! My life for his glory!

VOICE OF FREDERICK

See, my prison wall of childhood grows,
Surrounds a world wherein I rage;
Shriek with me now, my friends and my foes,
Aborted spawns of this deadly age.
Upon the rotten corpses mount we up
To drink the family poison from the cup.

(Above them the screens are alive with carnage. We see torn flesh, broken bones, skulls, skeletons. We hear a cold wind, a crackling of flames, and the low, steady murmur of a river of human voices, a quiet, blurred sound of anguish, streaming through time. Enter Frederick, still reciting. The cabinet stares at him. He recites grandly, as if playing a tragedy on a gilded stage. He is much older now, almost the grotesque figure we knew at the beginning of the play. The horrors on the screens continue.)

FREDERICK

Thanks to heaven my sorrows now exceed
All earthly expectation: oh, high praise,
You gods, for savage and unending skill.

GENERAL   *(Quickly)*   Sire, the capital has fallen. The Army is in chaos!

FREDERICK

Your hate rejoices in my misery,
You crown my wretchedness with great delight;
I was born to be a monument of your rage,
Of Sorrow the final, ultimate, finished work.

BISHOP *(Quickly)* Your Majesty, the people are beggars, picking their way through the wreckage of your kingdom! Something *must* be done!

FREDERICK

> Very well, I die content, all things fulfilled.
> But what thick night now wraps me round?
> What horrors shiver through my flesh?
> God! What rivers of blood flow all about me?

(He breaks off suddenly, smiles at everyone.)

Perfection, isn't it? That was Orestes, in Racine's *Andromache*. I've been reading it all night. No one compares with Racine, and the difference is character, simple character. I've been stealing verses from the wrong man all these years. Voltaire, that deadly bastard, has a detestable character, Racine was a faithful, upright man, and there's the difference. The mysteries of art and personality. Fascinating, yes?

(He mutters verses to himself.)

GENERAL Your Majesty, the Russian Army is in Berlin. Cossacks are burning the palaces, and slaughtering the people.

(Frederick mutters verses.)

LIEUTENANT If your Majesty wishes to end his life now, I will serve him before I serve myself. It will be for others to make the peace!

FREDERICK Make peace? Commit suicide? I see. Some grand law of fateful retribution has come round at last and we are all to be punished. Is surrender your consensus, gentlemen?

ALL It is, Sire!

FREDERICK   Then you would throw away a fatherland,
my dear friends and faithful advisers. I have a piece
of news for you, do listen. That vile bitch, the Empress
Elizabeth of Holy Russia, well, she has exhausted
and depleted all the men on earth and she has just
taken it into her head to die—so she could search out
more lovers in the kingdoms of hell. She's down there
now, prowling about, and little Peter is czar. He has
just sent me a charming note saying he loves me. Wor-
ships me. That immense Russian Army you think is
ready to destroy us *will defend us!* That is the way *that*
works, gentlemen. We've won. Again. Saved, all of us.

*(They gape at him. His irony now is furious. He has
reached its fullest intensity, and his emotion now is perhaps that of a Lazarus who did not want to be resurrected.)*

FREDERICK   What? No rejoicing? Just because salvation
comes out of this bizarre accident, should we not give
thanks all the same? Well, I don't blame you. For what
has saved us, do you think?

*(He pounds himself on the chest with mock-heroic blows,
struts about in a frenzy of self-loathing.)*

This! This fool of a fop! This madman! Peter adores me,
dreams about me, *prays* to me! His uniform, his personal guard, all just like mine! Now he's czar of Russia! Don't you understand? The man is crazy. Not just
odd, but a full-blown lunatic. He drills his soldiers in
Prussian drill but he drills cats, too. He court-martialed
one once, and executed it himself, on a tiny gibbet!
Cats! It's perfect. What a diabolical artist Life is, after
all. Somehow I manage to live all these years hanging
on to my sanity by my fingernails and now lunatics
swoon at my feet! Oh, God, a fool can always find
a bigger fool to fall in love with him! Well? Pre-

pare for a new round of alliances, and quite a few more years of this enchanting human life. Play the "Victory March," dust out the churches, get the priests moving with the Thanksgiving celebrations! Good afternoon!

(They leave him. He stands waiting. Now the soldier who always comes to him after a victory enters slowly.)

FREDERICK   I have been expecting you.

SOLDIER   Here is a letter from Voltaire, your Majesty. Written just before his death, which I regret to inform you has occurred.

FREDERICK   No, that's not possible. I wrote him last week that he would live to dance on my grave and write filthy verses about me. That his terrors were only funny, like all his other jokes.

(He takes the letter and reads it. Upstage we see Voltaire, very old now, leaning on a stick, bent over, but with a light still shining in his carbuncle eyes.)

VOLTAIRE
Sire:
    I am greatly consoled to know that my death agony amuses you. It is entertaining that at eighty-four I have escaped so many fatal illnesses. That is the advantage of being devoted to you. I drop your name and I get a little preference.
    All that is left to me now is to salute the man I loved, and not the bloody warrior who ravaged our century. You think, no doubt, that carnage is inevitable, and in the hands of the gods. No, Sire. It is not. Yesterday, at the production of my new tragedy, I saw a new public, a spirited people filled with hope, madly cheering verses that called the political saints of the past what they really were: superstitious tyrants.

And so you are wrong, and it is really true that in the end men do become enlightened. Tyrants cannot always blind them, and a new age of hope lies just ahead of us.

May Frederick the Great become Frederick the Immortal. Be graciously pleased to accept the final respects and unbreakable attachments of

Voltaire

(He vanishes.)

FREDERICK   You fool. Not to be ashamed of humanity. After all your work, you die like a trusting child, and cannot face the truth. Did he die with the priests, as I always said he would?

SOLDIER   He signed an article of faith, so he could be buried in a churchyard.

FREDERICK   Revolting. A ditch would have been nobler. And fitting, really. No one asks us whether we wish to be born into this life. We are put here. God knows why. We suffer in the spirit and in the flesh. We die without knowing why we were forced to march through life, why we must bear so much cruelty. Then we sink into nothingness, still resenting the futile role we have been obliged to play on this mysterious, shabby planet. Voltaire, Voltaire. We are judged not by our motives, but by our success. The only thing left to do is achieve it. The world will always believe the worst of us, and it is quite right.

(His eyes fill up with tears. He stands very straight.)

We are malevolent animals, as God made us.

(The wooden horse looms above him.)

There is nothing worse than a man.

(Blackout. Drums. The galloping shadow appears on the screen. Frederick goes off after the wooden horse, and offstage he mounts it and becomes again the Frederick of the first act.

A giant, a man seven feet tall, huge and shambling, comes onto the stage. He is dressed in tattered rags, is quite old, and has a dirty beard. The necks of several bottles are stuck into his fists, and he carries them about that way. He is bellowing and moaning, accosting imaginary passers-by with obscene hostility. He stops, stands still a moment, thinks through some grotesque thought to a conclusion, waves his arms, laughs, sits down, and arranges his bottles around him in a circle. Behind him, Frederick on his wooden horse moves closer. The giant begins to chant a warped song of his own, that reminds us of the patriots' hymn sung in the Tobacco Parliament, but now unmetrical, awkward, a war song long ago twisted around to suit his thoughts.)

GIANT *(Chanting)*
> Ride away, for the nights are cold,
> Ride away, for the days are hot,
> Ride away, for the wars are over,
> Far away, let the skeletons trot.
>
> But sing and be joyful, good soldiers,
> Sing and be joyful, every man here,
> Sing and be joyful, open your throats,
> Sing and be joyful, give us a cheer.
>
> And before we go, one gesture,
> Before we go, one sign,
> Before we go, stand up and sing
> One song that is loud and fine.
>
> Then hurray for the love of our country,
> Hurray for the faith of our wives,
> Hurray for the smiles of little babes,
> Hurray for the end of our lives.

Ride away, for the nights are cold,
Ride away, for the days are hot,
Ride away, for the wars are over,
Far away, let the skeletons trot.

(Frederick's horse is next to him. Frederick stands in his stirrups and peers down at the immense human wreck beneath him.)

FREDERICK   *(Gently)*   My friend, you will have to move yourself. Pick up your bottles and get drunk on the side of the road.

GIANT   And why should I do that? Ride around me if you don't like me. But don't touch my bottles. If you do, I'll break your neck. I'll tear your horse apart, too. I can do that if I want to. I'm old but I'm still strong.

FREDERICK   I'm sure you are. But you must move. There isn't room to ride around you, and the King is coming this way. He must pass, you know.

GIANT   The King? No, no, the King is dead. Died forty years ago, and more. I know, I was in his service. He died, and I was thrown out. I was a young man, then. In the Royal Potsdam Guards. Maybe you remember us. We were all seven feet tall or taller. The King loved us. We were his favorites. He had us kidnapped when we were boys. From all over the world. I was from Poland. Somebody saw how tall I was, and they kidnapped me and sold me to the King of Prussia. Maybe you remember. We were famous.

FREDERICK   I remember you very well. I used to drill with you.

GIANT   Oh? What did you think?

FREDERICK   You frightened me.

GIANT   *(Laughing)*   Did we?

FREDERICK   Yes. I did not like soldiers then. Especially soldiers seven feet tall, and I was afraid of you.

GIANT   Some were taller, you know. Yes, we were something to see.

(He points at one bottle after another, finally picks one, and drinks.)

FREDERICK   All the same, you'll have to move. Otherwise the King's guard will run you down. You remember what is was to be a soldier. You have to do what you're told.

(The giant lurches to his feet. He is a frightening figure, imposing in the harsh, articulate senility of his uncontrolled thoughts.)

GIANT   Remember? Yes, I remember. What else do I have to remember? I'll tell you the truth: it's the only thing I can remember. I'm over seventy years old. I've been wandering around trying to die, you see, but I can't. I get drunk and fall in a ditch and say, that's the end, that's the finish, but then daylight comes, and my old whirring brain hears a bugle blow, a trumpet sound, and I'm up, staggering around again. I can't help myself.

FREDERICK   How have you stayed alive?

GIANT   Can't remember that. I must have done something. Worked here and there, pushing, hauling, carrying things, I suppose. What place was there for me? Seven feet tall, a soldier of the King? I don't know what I've been doing. There were women, of course, a wife even, and a child, I think. I can't remember them. All I remember is bugles and straight lines, and the commands of the field. Polishing my rifle until the barrel gleamed. Scraping my bayonet until it caught the sunlight like a mirror. All that was over forty years ago, but I can't forget it. It was so simple, you see, and good. A good life. I have been staggering around for forty years afterward, poisoning myself, trying to die. But every morning the bugle blows in my brain, I am resurrected again, I go here, go there, try to find something good to do, but all I can think about are the commands. None come. Once I thought I heard a command and I killed an ox with a scythe. There was a lot of blood, and you can believe the farmer didn't like it. Well, I killed him, too, before I left. But you said you didn't like soldiers. I must be repulsive to you. All soldiers are, without commands.

FREDERICK   No. I am a soldier myself.

GIANT   Then you know what I'm talking about.

FREDERICK   Yes.

GIANT   Did you drill in the mornings? When it was fresh and the day was clear, and you could hear the commands sing in the air?

FREDERICK   Sometimes.

GIANT   Wasn't that wonderful? Wasn't that brave? I dream about it every night. Seventy years old, but I still dream about it. But who now will command me? To whom do I hire myself out? What wars do I serve? Where are the liars I must worship?

(The giant bellows military drill commands, and executes them, spinning himself about, lurching, almost falling, using a bottle for a rifle. Sharply, Frederick calls him to attention, and he stands erect, staring at the King.)

FREDERICK   As you were.

(The giant obeys him.)

FREDERICK   Now, listen. The King must pass. And really, he will be very interested to see you, standing guard over his back roads all these years. He will know what happened to you, even if you do not. That you were kidnapped, and torn away from yourself, for so was he. That you were drilled into slavery and forced to love what terrified you, until there was little room inside you for anything else. And that now, old as you are, you can never forget any of it, neither can he, he has lived a victim just as long as you; your image is very familiar to him. And now, if you will stand firm as he passes, and salute as you should—for he has his duties and his griefs, too; he is the King—well, he will command his soldiers to give you, finally, your reward for all this service.

(The wooden horse moves back a few feet, then stops.)

FREDERICK   Are you ready?

(The giant gapes at him. Tears come to his eyes.)

GIANT   The King?

FREDERICK   The King.

(The giant bellows himself to attention. The horse moves slowly past him, and the two ancient soldiers salute

*each other gravely. As the horse moves away, the giant
starts to weep and smile and hold out his arms like a
child. The horse moves out of sight, and we hear Frederick's harsh command. A tremendous fusillade of rifle
fire resounds, the giant is knocked backward by a hail
of bullets. The great body collapses. Blackout. Then a
small spot on the horse and Frederick, moving upstage.
We hear the giant's voice, as from far away, as it resounds in Frederick's mind.)*

VOICE OF THE GIANT
    Then hurray for the love of our country,
    Hurray for the faith of our wives,
    Hurray for the smiles of little babes,
    Hurray for the end of our lives.

    Ride away, for the nights are cold,
    Ride away, for the days are hot,
    Ride away, for the wars are over,
    Far away, let the skeletons trot.

*(The horse moves about the stage. The Lieutenant comes
out again to meet the King, and they stand once more
in the ancient positions of the Prince and Hans Katte.)*

LIEUTENANT   Your Majesty.

FREDERICK   Young man. Thank you for coming to meet me.
Now stand out of my way.

LIEUTENANT   Your Majesty, the funeral has already taken
place. I did not dream you would leave the field and
come back. Believe me, Sire.

FREDERICK   I believe you. Move.

LIEUTENANT   But the soldiers are digging up the coffin. How
can I serve you now? How can I spare you such torment?

FREDERICK   You can't. You can remind me of the children who were young and pliable, and not yet cast in iron, but you cannot help me. Get out of the way.

LIEUTENANT   I beg you. Let me stand between the King and his sorrows.

FREDERICK   Chick, he will ride you down.

(The Lieutenant steps back. Drums. The horse moves to the center of the stage. The shadow on the screen comes to rest and fades. The two soldiers enter, carrying an ornate but very small coffin. Without taking his eyes from the coffin, Frederick dismounts, faces the soldiers. With his back to us, he opens the coffin delicately and takes from it a small body, wrapped in a light-blue satin winding sheet. The soldiers leave. Silence. He stands, back to us, alone, embracing the corpse. He hears voices, faint, far off.)

VOICE OF VOLTAIRE   And so, if I have gained some authority in the world, it is as a cynic, who mocks belief. But let me tell you what I hope you already know. I play at cynicism, to make oppression ridiculous. I make my jokes and toss my acid all about me, but I avoid like the plague that true and sincere cynicism from which the word itself is coined.

VOICE OF A YOUNGER FREDERICK   Instruct me, as always. What word?

VOICE OF VOLTAIRE   A Greek word, Sire. *Kunikos.* It means canine, doglike. No longer human, if you will. It is a dreadful fate. I know of none worse.

VOICE OF A YOUNGER FREDERICK   Oh, come now, I can think of several. And I have just been given a litter of greyhound bitches; they're charming. They at least do not tell me lies and deceive me. They play at my feet, and adore me. No Madame de Pompadour would be so inexpensive, or so faithful. Now then, when are you coming to live with me?

(The voices have faded. On the screens at the side appear the face of the young Prince, done just before he became the King, a portrait by the court artist Pesne. The young, vibrant face looks down from both sides as Frederick the Great, old and withered, turns to us under these staring eyes of his youth, and moves downstage. In his arms he holds the dead and decomposing body of a dog, one of his many Italian greyhound bitches, whom he named Frolic. He embraces her, never taking his eyes from her face. He stares at her, as his youth stares down at him, then sinks to his knees, collapsing not so much in grief as in a fall of some last bastion of his spirit.

We hear Frederick's music: the slow, lyrical duet for two flutes from his Symphonia in D. On the screens, in rhythmic succession, appear visions of the bizarre figure in the three-cornered hat, walking in his palace gardens with his dogs. We see them jump beside him and eat from his hand. We see Frolic's aristocratic face nuzzling his boot. We see her eyes lifted up to him in love and devotion. The melodies of the two flutes soar, and they blend with the slow rasp of his croaking voice.)

FREDERICK   Why did you leave me? Oh, my darling. You were so young and so beautiful. I thought you would outlive me, my angel. You were to be curled on your rug at my deathbed. I meant to die with my eyes on your wonderful face, with the touch of your tongue and the warmth of your breath on my cheek. It was your love alone that was to be the extreme unction of the philosopher-King. But you left me, and went away, didn't you? Didn't you?

(He weeps.)

Oh, none of your sisters ever matched you. And you are still the angel of my delight, Frolic. Frolic! Your grandmother once was captured by the Austrians. Did you know that? Well, she was. And I could do nothing about it, though I would have torn open the universe to get her back. Then one day, while I was buried in maps and papers, deciding this and signing that, some officer, who had somehow got her back, simply brought her into my tent and let her loose without telling me. And she came barking to me and jumped in my lap, upsetting the papers of war, and fell into my arms. I wept then for her, as I weep now for you, and the Army and the Empire and the destinies of nations and all the philosophies of mankind were nothing to me then, as they are nothing to me now.

(He howls and clutches his throat. He sobs and becomes quiet again. The flutes play, beautifully.)

And you, when you were young, hopping about for a lump of sugar, making a mockery of all the great of my world who trooped in to tell me lies and deceive me. You never did that. You simply romped at my feet and would not let me be serious. You have outgrown all that wonderful foolishness now, my blessed darling. How composed and calm you are. How can you do it even now, assure me that in death all is well? You do, though. Even now, you love me and comfort me.

(His grief surges up in a vomit of sobs and moans. The flutes soar.)

In your arms at night, warm in our bed, our two little heads on one pillow, we gave ourselves up to each other, you and I, and I slept the only decent, sweet sleep of my life. In your embrace, my blessed angel, I lived the childhood I never knew, and, entwined with you, possessed all my freedom. Don't leave me! Come back! Frolic!

(The flutes are silent.)

But now you have already been under the dirt. You are beginning to rot. Good-by, my angel. You, at last, are my only philosophy. Wherever it is you are now, there do I wish to be. Hop about, and wait for me. I will come to you soon, and we will play in the fields of oblivion.

(With great care, and with exquisite agony, he covers the face of the dog with the satin winding sheet, sits back, makes a motion with one hand. The soldiers appear with the coffin, take up the body, and leave. Frederick remains on his knees, staring into the darkness. The Lieutenant appears behind him.)

FREDERICK   Yes?

SOLDIER   Your Majesty, the Army has been attacked. The General sends you this plea to give him his orders.

FREDERICK   *(Without looking)*   All right. I order him to destroy the enemy. Kill every man.

(The soldier leaves. Frederick stands motionless. We hear the faint sounds of the "Victory March." The sky turns red. Frederick heaves a great sigh of relief.)

FREDERICK   War.

(He wheels about and starts toward his horse, but suddenly, as if of its own volition, the wooden horse begins to move backward, away from him, and it slides off the stage. Enter the cabinet, arranged like pallbearers, carrying Frederick's iron cot as if it is a coffin. They move to the center of the stage, set the cot down with a firm thump, and stare at him.)

FREDERICK   Oh.

(He sags, then moves slowly to the cot. With no particular gentleness, they strip off his hat, wig, uniform coat, boots, and he lies down on his deathbed.)

DOCTOR   A short rest, your Majesty. It will do wonders.

FREDERICK   Please don't make me sicker than I am. You know very well why I lie down now.

DOCTOR   I have watched you conquer your enemies before, when I was sure you could not do it. Death, with a hundred sickles in his fists, stood back in awe of your will. He will do so again.

FREDERICK   Stale imagery, my friend. You are a good doctor, but a miserable poet. But . . . would you say . . . I have shown some physical courage in my life?

DOCTOR   You faced your fate with a heroism unequaled since the Roman Empire fell into dust. Like Death, I am a professional man, like him, in your presence I feel nothing but awe.

FREDERICK   Very pleasant of you. And better imagery. Goodby.

DOCTOR   Your Majesty.

(He bows to Frederick and moves downstage, where he speaks directly to us.)

DOCTOR   When he died, his body had shrunk to the size of a child's. His fevers, sweats, and constrictions never relented. He insisted on purgatives seven or eight times a day that would have killed anyone else. And the

Royal Council of Prussian Physicians told you I was a liar. That the King was everything a man should be. But I was his doctor, and I tell you he was by surgery sexually mutilated, and that he died very hideously diseased. That he lived as long as he did was a miracle. That he died sane, incredible.

(Exit)

(The Chancellor goes to the King's cot.)

FREDERICK   Anything in the Treasury? Or has some friend of yours run off with everything while I lie on my back?

CHANCELLOR   No, no. Your wars were devastating, but your fierce administration to all details rebuilt the nation. The Treasury is sound. You balanced every account. To the last decimal, your figures tally.

FREDERICK   Try to keep it that way for a week, at least. Then continue to lie with that same finesse.

CHANCELLOR   I do not have to lie about the achievements of Frederick the Great.

FREDERICK   I am great in no respect. I was applied, like a brush. Good-by.

CHANCELLOR   Your Majesty.

(To us)

He was the greatest miser, anyway, ever to sit on a throne. The sweat he ran out of us all would have floated an Armada. When he died, the palace was empty, deserted. His so-called friends were all long dead, his page boys and lieutenants gone. Only the dogs ran up and down the beautiful corridors. For the funeral, there wasn't a clean shirt to be found in the entire palace. We had to borrow one from a valet to dress the corpse. We had to scrub the corpse for hours.

(Exit)

(The General goes to the cot.)

FREDERICK   Is there still an Army, General, or have you thrown it away?

GENERAL   No, Sire. We engaged their troops, our soldiers gave a great cheer, as if you had returned to lead them, the enemy faltered and fled at the first discharge of fire. Europe is still terrified of the power you have given to Prussia. You are the greatest soldier who ever lived.

FREDERICK   How refreshing vainglory is, even now. My poor father would sizzle with envy. Another fool, General, will come along soon, and steal all our little arrows. Prevent it as long as you can. Good-by.

GENERAL   Sire.

(To us)

At the end, the Army was a shell, made up of convicts, uprooted peasants, and male harlots. Only his extreme discipline, which got worse and worse, held it together. Men were condemned to rot in prison dungeons for the slightest mistakes. He had soldiers run through gauntlets for nothing. He hung them on trees and flayed off their skins. The only escape from the Army was suicide, to take it became commonplace. Those discharged received nothing. Many died of poverty in the streets of Berlin. And it was Germans he fought, for he lived his life in French; he despised his own people, he destroyed the Holy Roman Empire with his Austrian wars, and he shed the blood of his fatherland all over Europe. As a soldier, I say it was not war he waged, but fratricide. And in spite of the surface idolatry, when the people heard he was dead at last, there was nothing in the streets but a tremendous feeling of relief.

(Exit)

(The Bishop goes to the cot, holding a Bible.)

BISHOP   It is time, your Majesty, to prepare your soul for death, and for the eternal life to come.

FREDERICK   Put that thing away. I refuse to toss petitions into the void, and you have more important work to do. I am trusting you to execute the details of my burial, as stated in my will. My clothes are not to be removed. You will simply throw a mantle over me, and entomb me quietly, with no pomp or ceremony, in my garden with all my dogs. Is that understood?

BISHOP   Perfectly.

FREDERICK   Then I leave it to you. Your duty, remember. Don't fail me.

BISHOP   Never, your Majesty.

(To us)

We buried him, of course, with stupendously pompous ceremony, in the crypt of the Garrison Church at Potsdam. Without his dogs. But there is one other coffin in the crypt. His father's, naturally. There they lie, father and son, entombed forever.

(Frederick's eyes are closed. The last figure emerges slowly from the darkness and moves to his side. It is the Lieutenant, militant, ramrod straight, filled with a sublime devotion. He stares at his stricken hero, then speaks to us.)

LIEUTENANT   I am his child. He created my spirit and gave me his soul, in sacred trust. I died for him a thousand times, and I will do so again, on ten thousand battlefields. What would I be without him?

(One by one, they have left him. Frederick lies propped up on his brutal iron cot, attended only by the wooden-faced soldier. His tenacity is gone at last, and he lies swooning. He opens his eyes.)

FREDERICK   There. Look, oh look. What's that, outside the door?

SOLDIER   Where, your Majesty?

FREDERICK   In the hall. Oh, look. One of my greyhounds. Don't you see her?

SOLDIER   No, your Majesty.

FREDERICK   Yes, she's there. All alone. She's cold, and shivering. Here.

(With a feeble hand he pulls a blanket from his legs.)

Take this out there to her. Wrap her warmly.

(The soldier takes the blanket and goes. Frederick swoons. He begins to mutter to himself. In this state, his eyes now closed, he sees again the phantom that came to him in his sleep at the beginning of the play. He struggles to sit up further. He holds out his arms.)

FREDERICK   No? No? Not at all? Oh, there you are! Yes, yes, I see you. Come along, darling, come along. Come, come.

(Drums. He sinks back onto the pillows that hold him upright on the cot. He opens his eyes. With his head wrapped up in the grotesque white handkerchief, he lies staring, as the moment of his death overtakes him.)

The mountain is passed. We will do better.

(A large black curtain, which we have not seen before, descends.)

Epilogue

VOLTAIRE   I am sorry to exhaust you further, but allow me to inquire if anyone else wishes to stage this play. Do be cautious. His spirit is still potent. Do you desire theatrical glory and fat receipts, and will you present the play accordingly? Take care. He appeals so strongly to worshipers of success that your sympathy may end in eulogizing a tyrant. Do you condemn his nature, and wish to expose the damage he inflicted on mankind? Take care. In the face of his sorrows, you will seem shrill, polemical, and small. From two hundred years of dust, he still interferes with everything.

Never were a father and a son more unlike. Oh, yes, indeed. The walls of that sad palace he expanded to the borders of the Empire, then made war upon it, and ultimately brought it down in ruins. The story of Frederick the Great is the story of a life that was an echo louder than its source, of a man who committed a crime, who sought out its consequences in the cannon fire, hatred, and maledictions of Europe, and who withstood that punishment with horrible bravery. He is the hero of the damned. But, for those days when the spirit of his father was not too heavy upon him, for his peculiar, flashing charm, and for his stark private truthfulness, it is impossible not to forgive him, and thus betray the rights of man.

We wish you success in your reincarnations of him, but permit us to leave you in quiet possession of this interesting dilemma, and wish you good evening.